QUIET CONVERSATIONS

QUIET CONVERSATIONS

What God Wants You to Know About Him

KIM HARVEY BRANNAN

KHB Publishing

Copyright © 2022 Kim Harvey Brannan

All rights reserved. No portion of this book may be reproduced, stored in a retrieval system, or transmitted in any form or by any means—electronic, mechanical, photocopy, recording, scanning, or other—except for brief quotations in critical reviews or articles, without the prior written permission of the publisher.

ISBN: 979-8-9874388-0-0 (hardback), 979-8-9874388-1-7 (paperback), 979-8-9874388-2-4 (ebook)

Seattle, Washington
www.kimharveybrannan.com
Designed by Mary Ann Smith
Author Photo by Sarah Ingram
Printed in the United States of America

This book is dedicated to

John Barkley Brannan,

the love of my life, who quietly radiated the light
of God's goodness and faithfulness,
touching the lives of so many.

Table of Contents

Introduction...8

Chapter One
"I Long to be Close"..10

Chapter Two
"I Speak Often"...20

Chapter Three
"My Love is Boundless"...34

Chapter Four
"I Care About My Children"..................................46

Chapter Five
"I Am Always with You"...56

Chapter Six
"Lean on Me"...66

Chapter Seven
"My Mercies are New Every Morning"................74

Chapter Eight
"I Welcome Repentant Hearts".............................82

Chapter Nine
"I Keep My Promises"..90

Chapter Ten
"I See Inside Your Heart"...102

Chapter Eleven
"I Can Work with Anyone"..110

Chapter Twelve
"I Love to Celebrate!"...119

Chapter Thirteen
"I Am Enough"...124

Chapter Fourteen
I Make All Things New"..134

Chapter Fifteen
"My Peace is Priceless"...144

Chapter Sixteen
"I Want the Best for You"..154

Afterword...164

Introduction

The Bible is a hefty book. It can sometimes overwhelm or intimidate because of its sheer volume, archaic or obscure language and profound revelations. The Bible is comprehensive—it is comprised of sixty-six books, written by forty authors, over the course of sixteen hundred years, composed in both Hebrew and Greek.

Many people wish they knew more about God and the Bible, but sometimes the task feels daunting. If you have thought this, or felt similar sentiments, this book is for you. I want to make the process simple. My intent is to introduce you to God by sharing what I believe to be the most significant things He wants you to know about Him.

I have studied the Bible for over fifty years. My knowledge and understanding have grown as I have matured. I have lived through experiences, of great joy and delight, as well as heavy heartache and pain, that have convinced me that the Bible's universality and truth remain valid and timeless.

God reveals Himself to each of us in many ways. For me, I have personally come to know Him best by reading and analyzing the Bible. I have taught Bible Studies to adults for over thirty-five years, and nothing gives me greater fulfillment than to see someone discover a new spiritual truth. When we share God's wisdom with one another, we all benefit. We can expand our understanding of God's love and grace in new ways.

My lifelong journey of seeking to know God has blessed me with an ever-evolving relationship with Him. There are many dimensions to God's personality, His ways of engaging with people, and the desires of His heart. I have found that learning these many nuances is a primary way to unlock the mysteries of God, to enable us to know Him, and to connect with Him, at a deeper level. I believe this is the secret to living an abundant life.

In the chapters that follow, I will highlight how God has worked through history, since the beginning of time, illustrating His many aspects with stories from the Bible and my own life. I have included questions for reflection at the end of each chapter to help you think more deeply about your relationship with God. I passionately believe that God intends for everyday individuals, like you and me, to know Him in a personal way and experience His transforming love.

My heartfelt hope as you catch a glimpse into the personality of God is that you will experience the joy of drawing closer to Him. I pray that you will discover the peace that comes from living a life grounded in God's purpose and passion.

— Kim Harvey Brannan

CHAPTER ONE

"I Long to Be Close"

We use the word "close" in different ways. When a mover asks me, "How close do you want the end table next to the couch?" he is speaking about nearness in physical distance. When I proclaim, "She is special to me. I feel very close to her," I am referring to a degree of familiarity and fondness shared with a treasured friend. When a mother sheepishly admits, "My identical twins look and act so close that it is hard to tell them apart," she is referring to resemblance and connection.

The Bible is God's story for humankind. From cover to cover of this vast spiritual book, we see God affirming His desire to be close to us. Close as in physical proximity? Yes. Close in familiarity and fondness? Yes. Close in resemblance and connection? Yes.

In the story of creation, God made humans after He created animals. This tells me that although the animals played a role in the new world He fashioned, God longed for more. He craved a relationship with a being more like Him. Genesis declares, "Let us make man in our image, after our likeness."[1]

---
[1] Genesis 1:26. Unless otherwise noted, all biblical passages referenced are from the Revised Standard Version.

Animals are a beautiful part of creation, but they are led by instinct and lack the ability to think abstractly. As human beings, we innately sense the difference between our physical, emotional, and spiritual aspects. God gave us the gift of insight to recognize these distinct elements. We understand how these elements sometimes interconnect or overlap in our day to day lives.

Because God resides in Heaven and we live on Earth, we recognize from a young age that the physical distance between us is enormous. I feel very far away from God in this sense. Fortunately, He has taken deliberate steps throughout history to bridge this separation. The Old Testament has colorful examples illustrating how God longs to be close to us.

Early pagans believed in a variety of different gods of nature. Their understanding was that these gods created them and then once they were done with their work, they immediately released them into the Abyss. Clearly, this was not a close relationship between Creator and creature.

But in my understanding of the truth, the God of the Bible created the world, and He chose to remain actively involved in His creation. Our God desires to be an engaged, ongoing part of our lives. He longs to be close. How can we know this? Let's examine some of the many ways He shows us.

Physical Proximity

In Genesis, we see God walk with Adam and Eve in the cool of the day, talk with them, and enjoy their friendship. We see God remind Noah that He was near to him and his family after the flood when he placed a radiant rainbow in the sky. We see God make a covenant with Abraham, promising the gift of land and a long line of descendants. God's people no longer had to live like nomads; He gave them a place to call home and raise families. Through Abraham, God created Israel, a new spiritual nation. He challenged them, "I will make of you a great nation, and I will bless you, and make your name great, so that you will be laughter cause Him to shake his head with recognition? Do our tears cause Him to pause and look upon us with compassion?

We will have to wait until we get to Heaven to know for certain what physical characteristics we share with God. But here on earth, we can know assuredly that we share a strong resemblance with Him emotionally and spiritually. We share a profound connection. He fashioned us that we might become kindred spirits with Him. We think, feel, and wonder similarly to Him, and because of this kinship, our hearts are bound together in love.

God knows my deepest secrets, greatest moments, and most painful wounds. The Psalmist captures this special relationship we share with God:

> *"O Lord, you have searched me, and you know me. You know when I sit and when I rise; you perceive my thoughts from afar. You discern my going out and lying down; you are familiar with all my ways. Before a word is on my tongue, you know it completely, O Lord."*[8]

The Spirit of God soothes me when I am weary and need to be refreshed. He girded me with strength to care for an aging mother when I was sapped of physical energy after a long day of work. I glance at my Bible on the nightstand and remember the truths and promises of God that sustain me. I reflect upon the many answered prayers I witness daily in my life and the lives of many loved ones.

I feel God in the sunshine, and I feel Him in the wind. I see him in the face of a child and in the ocean waves that crash upon the shore. God is constant. He does not change. He is always near me, and we enjoy each other's company because we are close, so very much alike.

What does God want you to know about Him? That he longs to be close.

---

[8] Psalm 139:14.

He has gone to great lengths to demonstrate this to us since the beginning of time. In the New Testament, James, the brother of Jesus, shares poignant advice, "Draw near to God, and He will draw near to you."[9] Draw near. He is right beside you. You are not alone.

---

[9] James 4:8.

Questions for Reflection

* When do you feel closest to God?

* How do you recognize God's presence in your life?

* Have you ever had a sacred experience, like that of the author when she held her great niece, Sophie, for the first time? How would you describe it? Did you feel as though you were basking in holy awe or standing on holy ground? How did the experience help you grow in your faith?

* What ways can you try to seek feeling closer to God in your life?

CHAPTER TWO

"I Speak Often"

If God desires to be close to us, it naturally follows that He wants to communicate with us on a regular basis.

I am blessed to know a small group of individuals who make up my inner circle. These folks are friends and family members whom I consider my closest confidantes. We share hard-won wisdom with each other. We are honest and candid. We make each other laugh. We listen intently. We comfortably share our hopes and dreams, fears and struggles. Our conversations nourish our friendships and deepen our bonds.

Communication is the foundation of any vital relationship. Without it, silence can pull people away from one another, forging a wedge. Most therapists agree that the secret to a healthy relationship is frequent, open communication—as any couple who has stood the test of time knows. My parents were married for sixty-three years. When asked about the secret to a successful marriage, my father responded, "I love to tell my wife jokes and funny stories. She thinks I am very witty." My mother responded, "I laugh at my husband's stories and antics, even though they are not really that funny."

It is no different with God. He speaks frequently in order to maintain an active, dynamic relationship with us. I believe God speaks uniquely to each of us by connecting with our hearts, minds, and souls.

In the Old Testament, we see God audibly speak to His leaders such as Noah, Abraham, and Moses. In the New Testament, we see God become flesh in the life of Jesus Christ, His only son. We have twenty-seven books in the New Testament devoted to the teachings and words—direct communication—of Jesus. Reading these books is one of the keys to knowing God and hearing His voice.

The four gospels of Matthew, Mark, Luke, and John record the history of Jesus' life and ministry. Tucked deep within these books are stories about the friendships, travels, conversations, and encounters Jesus experienced while on Earth. In the gospels, we gain insights into both the significant and simple moments that filled Jesus' life.

When we accept the fact that Jesus is God himself in the flesh, then we begin to glimpse God's personality. As we read the words Jesus spoke, we begin to understand they reflect God. Reading the gospels illuminates the nuances and style of Jesus' communication skills. We get to see His special way of responding to situations and people. When we read the stories of Jesus, we expect him to behave one way, when he sometimes behaves in another. We anticipate his message to be presented in hushed tones of respect, but then are surprised when he makes bold, radical statements to the leaders among the religious elite.

The Gospel of John was written by the disciple who was Jesus' best friend. We would be hard pressed to find a more intimate, personal glimpse into the man Jesus. John knew more than most what Jesus was really like after the crowds had gone away. John shares how Jesus interacted with others. He writes how Jesus grew tired and weary, and how he sought solitude. John shares the issues that upset, angered, and frustrated Jesus. He tells how Jesus was sometimes lonely, sad, and hungry.

When John begins His gospel, he introduces Jesus to his readers using an interesting metaphor. He refers to his best friend as "The Word."[10] This has always intrigued me because John could have chosen any number of metaphors; yet he chose one that embodies communication. When we speak, we use words. When we listen, we hear language. And language is one primary facet that separates humans from the rest of God's creation. To John, Jesus was the essence of communication.

What is the function of words? Words have power. They reveal thoughts and provide information. They teach, inspire, warn, encourage, forecast, and engage. As "The Word," Jesus lived a life designed to communicate with those around him. God's purpose for sending Jesus to the world was to speak to us, to communicate our Heavenly Father's message of love and grace.

We are told in the first chapter of John's gospel, "No one has ever seen God; the only Son, Jesus, who is in the bosom of the Father, He has made Him known."[11] The way Jesus speaks, God speaks. The way Jesus thinks, God thinks. The way Jesus loves, God loves. He was the flesh and blood, walking and talking individual who showed us who God is and how He feels about us. Jesus makes God known.

The writer of Hebrews proclaims, "In many and various ways God spoke of old to our fathers by the prophets; but in these last days he has spoken to us by a Son, whom he appointed the heir of all things."[12] Because God chose Jesus to speak on his behalf, we know His words are true. What Jesus says is validated by God's stamp of approval. Just as God commissioned the prophets in the Old Testament to speak to His people for him, so He ordained Jesus to serve as His mouthpiece.

Do you speak to your mother the same way you address your co-work-

---

[10] John 1:1.
[11] John 1:18.
[12] Hebrews 1:1-2.

er? Of course not. We employ different communication styles based upon the type of relationship we have with our audience. When my children were young, I used to instruct them to choose their words carefully. I would warn, "Don't say anything you would not repeat in front of your grandmother." That usually warded off any inappropriate expressions or ugly words slipping from their tongues.

In terms of familiarity and respect, we speak in ways that make our listeners feel comfortable. I do not speak to a professional colleague in the same manner or style as I do with my brother. In like manner, I believe God speaks in ways that are unique to individuals. As our Creator, He knows us intricately. He meets us where we are.

God knows that my favorite color has always been blue. He often speaks to me when I spend time focusing on a bright blue sky or glance across a body of crystal blue water. I grew up on a lake, and I now live steps away from Tampa Bay and the Gulf of Mexico. My connection to water opens my spirit to hear him. Because I am a lover of Scripture, He often speaks phrases from the Bible to my heart.

God knows how to communicate His love, wisdom, and peace in ways that will resonate best with each believer. Do you seek to hear God's voice more frequently in your life? I encourage you to reflect and discover the specific ways you open your heart best to Him. What feels the most natural and comfortable to you? Reading the Bible? Listening to music? Spending time with faith-filled people whom you respect? Pray for God to quicken your senses and recognize His voice when He speaks.

I am a fan of the writings of Gary Chapman. In 1992, I read his timeless book The Five Love Languages.[13] It completely transformed my thinking about relationships. Chapman presents the idea that all individuals express and receive love in one of five primary ways, which he calls "love languages." They are

---

[13] Chapman, Gary, *The Five Love Languages*, Northfield Publishing, 1992.

words of affirmation, acts of service, gift giving, quality time, and physical touch. Through studying Chapman's book, I learned that my primary love language was words of affirmation, and my husband's was acts of service. It strengthened our marriage to learn how to express love to one another in the way that our spouse prefers to receive love.

Twenty years later, Chapman came out with another tremendous book, The Love Languages of God.[14] If his original book transformed my thinking, this book rocked my world! I came to realize that not only do people express their love in the language their partner prefers, but God does the same thing. He does not take a cookie-cutter approach in the way He speaks to believers. God expresses His love to me differently than the way He does to you. Why? Because the way I receive love is specific to me, and the way you receive love is specific to you.

This all makes perfect sense because God created each one of us to be unique. That is why no two fingerprints are alike. We all relate to different characteristics and aspects of God, we all communicate in our preferred style, and we all interpret life from our own perspective. Over the course of time, all our individual experiences impact how we know and relate to God. Naturally, God understands this, and He wants to adapt the way He speaks to each one of us to maximize our willingness to hear Him.

I am a lover of words. My career as a marketing director involved using words all day in written documents and oral presentations to communicate important messages about companies and their products and services. In my personal life, my two most passionate pursuits are reading and writing. My favorite game is Scrabble. I enjoy doing a crossword puzzle every day. Perhaps this is why God primarily speaks to me through the Bible, his written Word. He is speaking to me in my love language.

Before I explore any passage in The Bible, I always pray first, asking God

---

[14] Chapman, Gary, *The Love Languages of God*, Northfield Publishing, 2002.

to "Give me the eyes to see and the ears to hear the truth you would have for me." He never ceases to reveal Himself to me in this way. I come to know Him more intimately as I thumb through the pages and reflect upon His insights.

Conversely, others hear God's voice and sense His nearness more readily while they are gardening. Many feel his presence by taking a walk or listening to the howl of the wind. These individuals most likely receive love through quality time. Spending time in quiet reflection surrounded by God's creation opens their minds and hearts to hear Him speak. The Psalmist proclaims, "I lift up my eyes to the hills—where does my help come from? My help comes from the Lord, the maker of heaven and earth."[15] The writer of this beautiful song experienced the same joy of sensing God's presence while soaking up the wonder of His creation.

My Grandma Elsie used to love to go fishing on a small lake with her dear friend Katie. She counted these outings as some of her most cherished memories. When I was young, I asked her, "Grandma, what do you and Katie talk about when you fish?" She smiled patiently and replied, "Darlin' we don't say a word. We just sit and listen to God together."

I count it one of life's greatest blessings that I have been an active part of a church family that seeks to collectively hear God's voice. We share our burdens and concerns and pray for one another. I have learned there is great power in the fervent prayers of God's people.

When I pray about something very specific, I search the Scriptures, and God usually leads me to a particular passage, chapter, or section of The Bible. It never ceases to amaze me how this works, but it does. However, on occasion, I do not hear God's voice through Scripture. When this happens, I simply wait on God. After a period, He delights me by using other believers to deliver His message directly. Often, these individuals are not even aware that what they are sharing with me is the precise message I have been waiting to receive from God. But I

---

[15] Psalm 121:1-2

know the minute I hear it from their lips, and I smile in gratitude. God knows just what I need to hear from Him, precisely when I need to hear it.

God has long used others to speak on His behalf. We have many examples throughout both the Old and New Testaments demonstrating how God employed this strategy of communication. Following the exodus of the Israelites from Egypt, Moses was overwhelmed by the volume of people continuously coming to him, day and night, to resolve all their disputes and conflicts. Moses was frustrated and tired. He prayed, asking God for wisdom. One day his father-in-law, Jethro, visited and told him:

> *"What you are doing is not good, Moses. You will wear yourself out. You cannot handle this alone. Select capable men from among the people, those who fear God, trustworthy men who hate dishonest gain. Appoint them as officials over thousands, hundreds, fifties and tens. Have them serve as judges for the people at all times, but have them bring every difficult case to you; the simple cases they can decide themselves. This will make your load lighter because they will share it with you."*[16]

I can only imagine how elated Moses was that Jethro had come to visit. God knew that Moses would heed this wise counsel from his father-in-law whom he loved and respected. Jethro delivered the exact instructions and advice Moses needed at the right time. This new idea to delegate completely transformed Moses' leadership style and alleviated his stress. God repeatedly spoke to Moses through Jethro—and others, and it made a profound impact upon his life.

Sometimes God works through others to get our attention. It is as if He needs to hold our chin in his hands, to reach us face-to-face. I cannot count the

---

[16] Exodus 18:13-23. This story undergirds the importance of delegation by spiritual leaders. God does not expect us to be lone heroes but instead to organize ourselves so that our ministry and workload can be shared.

number of times that God has done this in my life through my steadfast friend Donna. We share our deepest thoughts and feelings with one another without judgment. We have weathered many of life's storms together. God continues to use Donna to speak His truth to me. Sometimes what she shares is hard to hear, but she holds me accountable and pulls me back when needed. She never speaks harshly, yet always in love.

My friend Kit is one of the wisest people I have ever met. She is very bright, and she possesses enormous common sense. I don't know how I would have gotten through college without her because she listened so carefully and talked me through so many situations. Today, we are separated by many miles, yet when I need her wisdom to help me discern a problem, or if I simply long to hear her enthusiasm and encouragement, she is only a phone call away.

How do I know it is God speaking through Donna and Kit? Because I never resent their words. I never become defensive or angry because they both speak calmly and bring clarity. Their words align with Scripture. Donna has a peaceful spirit, and her words overflow with sound, Godly wisdom. Kit has a no-nonsense approach to life, and everything in my being knows and trusts that her words are often God's words spoken directly to me. I am grateful that these precious friends have an open heart, keen spirit, and willingness to be used by God in my life.

In the Books of Acts, we learn about the journeys of the apostles in the early church. At times, Peter or Paul prepared to set out for a particular destination, but fellow believers advised them against it. Because the apostles' spirits were quickened to God working actively in their lives, they listened and changed course. They were grateful to heed God's direction.[17] Who knows what danger was averted because brave Christians shared with the apostles what God revealed to them?

God uses many channels to communicate with His children. Throughout

---
[17] Acts 21:1-6

the ages, God's artful hand pricks our hearts and stirs our souls through the gift of music. It can reach inside us to a place few other mediums can touch. Our emotions are easily affected by music. Sometimes God is felt in the crescendo of violins, in the sturdy beating of drums, or in the swell of voices. Perhaps this is why music is featured so prominently in worship services. It is an excellent way for us to offer our praise and thanks to God, and a great way for God to grip our hearts. If we listen between the notes and measures, we can hear God speak.

The Book of Psalms is the longest of the sixty-six books in The Bible. It contains 150 chapters, and each chapter contains a song, penned by different musicians. Many of these songs were written by King David who played a small harp. Some were written by Solomon, David's son who succeeded him as king of Israel. Others were written by Moses, and some were penned by anonymous authors. These beautiful songs span centuries and play an exceptional role in Scripture. They capture the full gamut of human emotion, reminding us that God wants to hear everything we think and feel, whether it is praise, gratitude, mourning, tears, confession, or joy. Some of our most poetic and beautiful Christian hymns draw inspiration from the Book of Psalms.

The Psalmist proclaimed:

"O come, let us sing to the Lord; let us make a joyful noise to the rock of our salvation! Let us come into His presence with thanksgiving, let us make a joyful noise to Him with songs of praise."[18]

If we are having a hard time getting into the proper mindset or attitude for worship, music can lift us out of ourselves. Music can remind us of the beauty and excellence of God and prepare our hearts to receive and hear His voice.

The Apostle Paul wrote, "Let the word of Christ dwell in you richly, teach and admonish one another in all wisdom, and sing psalms and hymns and spiri-

---

[18] Psalm 95:1-2.

tual songs with thankfulness in your hearts to God."[19] I cannot think of a lovelier picture of what the church of Christ looks like than this. It is a joy to encourage one another and share wisdom through singing and music. The Bible teaches that Heaven will be filled with angels singing in our eternal, celestial home.

The way God uses music in our lives is indeed a mystery. I am awed by how He uses it to draw me to Him. As my ears listen, my spirit soars. My heart opens, and I yearn to hear God's voice. The more He speaks, the more I long to hear. My heart cannot contain the enormity of it all. God fills me up with His love, and I feel like King David when he sang, "My cup overflows!"[20]

Music is but one of many art forms that God uses to speak to us. When I see the tender stroke of paint on a canvas or the masterful carving of a marble sculpture, I sense God's presence. When I watch a live performance of a play or witness ballerinas dancing gracefully, my spirit quickens, and I begin to hear God's voice.

Some of the most holy moments I have witnessed have been in non-traditional yet sacred places. Art museums move me in such a way that I prefer to visit them alone, to soak up the experience of the immense beauty. Gazing at a weathered, old desk in an antique store speaks to me of the lives who once sat there, waiting to be inspired, pen in hand. Wrapping myself up in a handmade quilt of my grandmother's, I hear God's whispers of grace, shared through the generations of my family.

I am also drawn to traditional settings, many which radiate God's holiness and awe. I have heard His voice speak anew to me in places where spiritual pilgrims have gone centuries before me. Years ago on a trip to Paris, my husband John and I visited the renowned cathedral, Notre Dame. Inside, we parted to explore this magnificent place individually. It was simply too sacred to share. I sat in a dimly lit alcove, with candles aglow, gazing up at the stunning stained

---

[19] Colossians 3:16.
[20] Psalm 23:5.

glass. I stared at a hand-carved, wooden statue of Jesus on the cross. I meditated on the inscription below that said, "Behold, the Lamb of God, who takes away the sins of the world," which brought to mind the words of John the Baptist when he first saw Jesus in the flesh.[21] In my heart, I felt that my sins were attached to the nails that held him. In that moment, I knew God was near. He poured His silent words of love and sacrifice into my soul.

John later shared with me that he was drawn to a tiny room mere steps away from the large sanctuary. This was an area where worshippers went to request prayer for specific circumstances and special needs in their lives. Most were handwritten, in large bound books, with updates added later to tell how the prayers were answered or the needs were filled by members of the church. This moved John immensely. My husband's primary love language was acts of service, so naturally God led him to this small, sacred spot in Notre Dame where He witnessed the power and grace of service by God's people.

Experiencing God's beauty in a variety of ways helps me to listen and hear His voice more acutely. I believe that the Apostle Paul grasped this mystery when he instructed believers to do the following:

> *"Finally, brothers, whatever is true, whatever is honorable, whatever is just, whatever is pure, whatever is lovely, whatever is gracious, if there is any excellence, if there is anything worthy of praise, think about these things."*[22]

Prayer is a time when we clear our minds, focus on God, and meditate on these worthy things. Prayer can be an important practice to hear God's voice, but we can only hear God speak when we stop talking and begin to listen. Prayer is designed to be a dialogue, not a monologue.

---

[21] John 1:29.

[22] Philippians 4:8.

What does God want you to know about Him? That He speaks often. Are you listening? Whatever it takes, open yourself up to Him. Listen and ponder His words. There is nothing in the whole world like hearing His voice.

Questions for Reflection

* Do you hear God speak to your heart, mind and soul? What circumstances, or times in your life, do you feel most open to hearing His voice?

* What sometimes prevents you from hearing God's voice?

* Has God ever spoken to you through another individual? How did you know it was His voice coming through them?

* What elements in your life create a strong, healthy environment for you to be open to hearing God speak?

CHAPTER THREE

"My Love is Boundless"

There are probably more songs written about love than any other subject. All you have to do is put on a Spotify playlist to hear different versions of multiple artists and their renditions on love. Often what makes for compelling lyrics is similar to what makes sizzling soap opera scripts—cheating hearts, falling in and out of love, and broken lives. We humans have found every possible way to take something as precious and meaningful as love and mess it up.

Fortunately, God's love is completely foreign to the kind of love we know and experience daily as human beings. Whereas our love is limited and often falls short, God's love does not. His love is boundless.

The word "boundless" means "having no boundaries; infinite; vast; unlimited." This is my favorite word to describe God's love because there are no limits. His love is larger and vaster than our minds can comprehend. God's love is fuller and more immense than any boundary can contain. Our finite minds cannot grasp such an infinite concept. It simply overwhelms our imagination.

Another word to describe God's love is "bounteous," which means "given freely; liberally bestowed; plentiful and abundant." This is how God dispenses His love—bounteously, without restraint. God never runs out of His love; there is always more to give. It is not like a gas tank in a car that will eventually run dry if it is not refilled. God's love is like a natural, flowing stream; it is a fountain that never stops gushing with fresh, new water.

I have enjoyed knowing deep love from many people in my life, but the person who has demonstrated the most bounteous love to me, over the course of my lifetime, is my brother Rick. As a career airline pilot, Rick knew and understood the concept of "vastness" as he flew high above the clouds each day. He once shared with me how moved he was when he was flying, glimpsing what seemed to be endless air and clouds above the earth. Rick got tears in his eyes as he shared that this view was a visual reminder of the immensity of God and His love. Rick lived large. Everything he thought, did and said, he did with pure abandon. He loved lavishly until the day he died this past year, leaving a tremendous void for our family. The texts he used to send me constantly shared how much he loved me and how proud he was to have me as his sister. His love always made me feel like a million bucks. Rick's love was the closest human demonstration of how God loves that I have ever known.

In his first epistle, the disciple John wrote a succinct statement, one that has been pondered through the ages: "God is love."[23] These three words pack a punch. Perhaps we have made it more complicated than it really is, but I believe it is impossible to know God without knowing His love. God's love is an intrinsic part of who He is—I believe this is what the Apostle John is saying.

However, to say that "God is love" is not to say that the inverse is also correct, that "Love is God." This is not like algebra where if A=B, then B=A. I assert that it is not our understanding of love that defines God, but rather God's actions toward us that define what real love is. John explains, "This is love, not that we loved God but that He loved us and sent His son as an atoning sacrifice

---

[23] I John 4:7-8.

for our sins."[24]

If our finite minds defined love, it would be limited. And God's love has no limits. When I was young, we had a neighbor who raised bunnies. I distinctly remember the first time I visited his back yard, I gasped when I caught sight of the most adorable creatures I had ever seen. Their long, floppy ears were precious. Their soft fur felt like cotton. Their blue eyes and pink noses sparked a sense of magical wonder for me. Because of how I felt about them, I thought that bunnies were the equivalent to love. In high school, I dated a young man for two years. It was my first experience of real, romantic love. I thought what we shared was the foundation of love. But neither of these experiences adequately determine love. As the disciple John shared, it is God's efforts on our behalf that make Him the embodiment of love—and allow us to say with confidence that "God is love."

I have a wonderful friend, Jill, who enjoys introducing her closest friends to each other. She always says, "I love to share my friends." She has done this for me many times through the years, and I am always grateful for the new friends I have made. Jill usually starts by describing the qualities she enjoys about a friend I have not met. Then, over time, I am hooked. I beg to meet them. This kindness on her part has been a lovely way to expand my circle of friendships.

I suppose my relationship with God is a lot like how Jill feels about her treasured friends. I want to share His attributes and qualities with others so that they, too, can come to know Him and experience His love. It is so easy to introduce God to others because His many characteristics are like a magnet drawing people to Him. Let us explore some of these together.

God's Love Initiates

God makes the first move in our relationship with Him. We see this from

---

[24] I John 4:10.

the beginning of creation when He chose to make us. We continue to see His proactive hand in history as His people grow and evolve. Moses wrote to remind the people of God's initiating love for them:

> *"The Lord your God has chosen you out of all the peoples on the face of the earth to be His people, His treasured possession. The Lord did not set his affection on you and choose you because you were more numerous than other peoples, for you were the fewest of all peoples. But it was because the Lord loved you."*[25]

After I graduated from college, I joined a new church. The church I grew up in no longer existed, and so it was time to find my own way with a new congregation. I found a Presbyterian church, which I loved, and I continue to be an active member. This special church is where I met my husband, the place we were married, presented our three children for baptism, and where we knew the joy of witnessing our children's confirmation of faith.

When I first started attending, it was quite a change for me because I was not raised in the Presbyterian denomination. My background was more legalistic, and I found the emphasis on God's grace and bountiful love refreshing. The spiritual upbringing of my childhood practiced baptism by immersion after an individual came to the full knowledge and acceptance of Christ as his or her Savior. The practice of infant baptism observed by the Presbyterian church was new to me, but it has become one of the sacraments I treasure most in our denomination.

The Old Testament premise behind infant baptism resides in the concept that God takes the first step in our relationship with Him. When each of our children were baptized, John held our sweet baby in front of the baptismal font as we publicly affirmed that God had already called and chosen our child to

---

[25] Deuteronomy 7:7-8.

know Him and experience His love. We were offering our child to God, hoping that by His grace and love that John Jr., Mark, and Laura would each one day come to know and trust Jesus as their Savior. Not the other way around!

God's grace initiates salvation. God's love calls our name before we ever learn how to think or speak on our own. As a tiny infant, God loves each one of us for who we are—a miracle, a child of His, designed to grow and learn of His mighty, powerful love. Acknowledgment and acceptance of this initiating love by God is a deep, meaningful act to celebrate in our faith.

God's Love Is Universal

The Apostle Paul wrote to encourage Timothy, a young pastor, by reminding him of the outstretched arms of God's love, "God desires all men to be saved and to come to the knowledge of the truth."[26] Never doubt that God desires to know you. God welcomes all.

Most children blessed to be raised in a faith-filled home have most likely learned, and perhaps memorized in Sunday School, the foundational Bible verse found in John 3:16. It is a treasure indeed as it promises eternal life to all who believe. The verse that immediately follows it in the gospel undergirds God's universal love, "For God sent the Son into the world, not to condemn the world, but that the world might be saved through Him."[27] God's love is universal. His heart longs to save everyone in the world, the very world that He fashioned from dust and bountifully loves.

When adults who did not grow up with a faith tradition become Christians, it brings an entirely new dimension to their lives. They begin to look at the world through a different lens. They question things they had never previously pondered. All aspects of faith feel new. Beginning to learn Scripture for the first

---

[26] I Timothy 2:4.
[27] John 3:17.

time as an adult is a different encounter than that of a child. With intellectual development and the maturity of life's experiences, concepts are more easily digested and often more enlightening. Some of us who grew up in families deeply rooted in the Christian faith can sometimes take spirituality for granted, whereas adult converts usually do not.

God's Love Is Faithful

In today's world, it is hard to find someone who will be 100% faithful as a spouse, friend, or employer. I am sure there are many reasons why this has changed over the past fifty years, but I suppose it might relate to how costly faithfulness is to the person who chooses to be faithful. Our society has become so self-centered that perhaps faithfulness just costs too much of ourselves.

To be faithful to a spouse, we need to place their needs over our own. Ouch! That's tough. We really care about our own needs. To be faithful to a friend requires us to keep confidences and show up for our friends even when we are tired or stressed ourselves. That's not always easy. For an employer to remain faithful to an employee, they might have to part with money they had not planned to give away. No one likes eating into their profits. To be faithful will always cost something.

God's love is faithful. He never withholds it, despite how sinful His created ones can be. His faithfulness is rooted in how unconditionally He gives His love. God never tries to trick or manipulate us with His love—he never says, "I will love you if…" God never uses His love as leverage to get something He wants.

Years ago, I taught Sunday School to preschoolers with my dear friend Diane. We only taught for one year because it was a very challenging age group. The questions that arose from the little ones never seemed to end. We kept our lessons simple so that with hope, and a lot of prayer, the children would at least learn one thing by the end of the year. Diane and I were not overachievers. We really only wanted to teach them one thing—God loves you.

I cannot count the number of times the children would respond to that all-important truth by looking at us with their big, round eyes, asking "Why?" Week after week, the only answer that seemed to make any sense to us was, "Just because. God loves you because you are you." Years later, when I reflect upon that experience, I still believe in that same answer. God loves us simply because we are His. That is faithful love.

The prophet Jeremiah spoke for God, reminding the people that the Lord had not forsaken them, "I have loved you with an everlasting love; therefore, I have continued my faithfulness to you."[28]

God's Love Is Reconciling

The word "reconcile" means "to restore to harmony; to settle; to resolve conflict." Genuine love never looks the other way when troubles arise. Authentic love always goes through a difficulty, never around it.

God's love is a forgiving love that leads to reconciliation. Within the first three chapters of The Bible, we learn that humans made poor choices when given the gift of free will. When Adam and Eve chose disobedience over following God's way, sin was born. Being fully human, we inherited the propensity for sin. We often choose wrong over right, evil over good, and the way of the world over God's higher path. From that day in the garden, sin erected a wall between us and God, blocking the harmony in our relationship with Him.

Despite its wretchedness, even sin does not change God's love for us. Rather, our sinfulness is met by God with abundant forgiveness. The Apostle Paul passionately addressed this:

> *"But now in Christ Jesus, you who once were far away have been brought near through the blood of Christ. For he himself is our*

---

[28] Jeremiah 31:3

peace, who has made the two one, and has destroyed the barrier, the dividing wall of hostility."[29]

An aspect of God's reconciling love that cements our restored relationship is that His forgiveness is permanent. Unlike in human relationships, He doesn't bring our past sins up and throw them in our face to shame us every time we repeatedly stumble. Rather, God loves us unconditionally, forgiving and forgetting our sin. He chooses to forget our past errors.

The Bible tells us that David knew a lot about sin—grave, serious sin. Even though he is remembered as the greatest king of Israel, David committed adultery, murder, and deception. His life teaches us that the lower we fall, the more willing God is to reach down and lift us up with His outstretched arms of mercy. David poured out his soul in the depth of his sin, sharing, "For as high as the heavens are above the earth, so great is His love for those who fear him; as far as the east is from the west, so far has He removed our transgressions from us."[30]

As David and countless others have learned, no sin is too big for God's grace. His boundless love is reconciling. He forgives and accepts us back into His presence with joy. God scatters our sins, never to be thought of again. He wipes our slate clean.

This is perhaps why Jesus told the parable of The Prodigal Son, a story about a slothful, ungrateful young man who broke his father's heart by asking for his inheritance early. The son left home and squandered the money in a foreign land with revelry and debauchery. After he lost everything, he came to his senses and returned home, head hung low, to ask his father's forgiveness. His father all the while had been waiting and watching for his son. When the son was yet at a distance from home, his father spotted his figure on the horizon. When he saw his lost son, he began to run, and when he met him, he embraced and kissed him.

---

[29] Ephesians 2:13-14, NIV.
[30] Psalm 103:11-12.

This story is the picture Jesus chose to paint of God's actions when we repent of our worst mistakes and most embarrassing blunders. As our Heavenly Father, God's reconciling love freely offers grace and forgiveness. He welcomes us with open arms and puts the past behind us, just like the father in the parable. With God's reconciliation comes celebration because a child who was lost is now found. This brings immeasurable joy to the father's heart. Just as in the parable, I believe an elaborate party is given in Heaven to celebrate, with jubilant dining and dancing, to honor each wayward child who returns home to receive God's reconciling love.

God's Love Is Transforming

The power of God's love is so strong and fierce that it not only forgives, but it transforms. An orphaned child's world is turned upside down when she is finally adopted, and her life is suddenly changed forever. She is no longer just a person—now, she is someone's child. She is someone who has parents who chose her, love her, and promise to always be there for her. We are just like this child. Because God has elected to redeem us, we are overwhelmed by the enormous extent of His love and grace that we yearn to live as His child. We are beloved and precious in His sight. Living as His children transforms us forever.

My daughter, Laura, has always loved butterflies. Growing up, her room was decorated with pretty butterflies on her wallpaper and nylon butterflies clipped to her window blinds. When she was twelve, she confirmed her faith at our church. She participated in a twelve-week class taught by our pastor, and at the conclusion, Laura made the decision to accept Jesus Christ as her Savior. She decided to make Him the Lord of her life. Our family was filled with joy for sweet Laura. To commemorate this milestone in her life, I made a plaque with a wooden butterfly as a gift to hang on her wall, painted with the following Scripture, "Therefore, if anyone is in Christ, he is a new creation; the old has passed away, behold, the new has come."[31]

When God's transforming love touches our life, we change from a clumsy caterpillar crawling on the ground into a beautiful butterfly with wings that help us soar.

I am certain that one of the greatest riches we will ever know is the love of God. The Apostle Paul tried, as we all do at some point in our lives, to wrap his mind around the immensity of God's love. His faith was grounded in the promise that we would never be without God's love, as he professed:

> *"For I am sure that neither death, nor life, nor angels, nor principalities, nor things present, nor things to come, nor powers, nor height, nor depth, nor anything else in all creation, will be able to separate us from the love of God in Christ Jesus our Lord."*[32]

What does God want you to know about Him? That His love is boundless. You will never have to know life outside His faithful love. My highest hope is that you will allow His love to transform and sustain you.

---

[31] II Corinthians 5:17.
[32] Romans 8:38-39.

Questions for Reflection

* Have you experienced the boundless love of God in your life?

* Have there been times when you were aware of the faithfulness of God's love? How did it make a difference in your situation?

* Can you describe a time when God's reconciling love changed the direction you were headed?

* How are you aware of God's transforming love in your life?

CHAPTER FOUR

"I Care About My Children"

The life, travels, and ministry of Jesus teach us a lot about God. Scriptures tells us that Jesus reveals God the Father to us. When asked about this mystery by his disciple Thomas, Jesus declared, "He who has seen me has seen the Father...I am in the Father and the Father is in me."[33] Jesus was like a mirror—he was the living, breathing embodiment of who God is—and his life shows us God's personality, attributes, choices, decisions, and reactions to people and circumstances. If we want to know what God is like, it is helpful to look at the life of Jesus.

In the New Testament, we meet Jesus and learn about His life from birth to death, from His resurrection to His ascension back to Heaven. We witness how Jesus engaged with religious leaders and with common, everyday folks. We hear Him laugh and see Him cry. We watch Him grow tired and weary. We sense his moments of delight, and we are awed when we see young children climb all over him, longing to snuggle.

One of the impressions I glean from the gospels is that Jesus cared

---

[33] John 14:10-11.

passionately about people and their needs. He cared about their thoughts and ideas, their questions and curiosities. Their health and wellness mattered to Him. He was sensitive to their feelings and emotions. When we see how Jesus cared about important elements in people's lives, we can be certain that God cares about them as well.

Does it astound you that the creator of the universe, who has such vast responsibilities and concerns for the world, takes time to care about how you are feeling today? That he wants to know why you are worried and anxious about tomorrow? He does. I am continually comforted to know that God cares about my pain and heartache, along with my joys and triumphs.

This is why it feels natural to refer to God as my "Heavenly Father." Each day He bestows His support and protection upon me, just as my extraordinary father and mother did my whole life. Jesus taught us about God's love in the way He lived, demonstrating genuine concern for others. The following examples represent the depth and breadth of His affection and thoughtfulness toward His children.

God Cares About Our Physical Health

During his ministry, Jesus frequently met people with various ailments, illnesses, and afflictions. When Jesus and his disciples were leaving Jericho, they saw a blind man begging on the side of the road. Sadly, this was a common sight. The man's name was Bartimaeus. As the disciples shuffled passed, he heard their small group address Jesus by name. Bartimaeus cried out, "Jesus, Son of David, have mercy on me!" The disciples criticized him and asked him to pipe down. Apparently, this only spurred Bartimaeus on, and he cried out louder, "Jesus, Son of David, have mercy on me!" Jesus stopped suddenly in his tracks. He asked the disciples to call the blind beggar over. When Bartimaeus rushed over, Jesus asked him, "What do you want me to do for you?" Without hesitation, he replied, "Master, let me receive my sight." Jesus said to him, "Go your way, your faith has made you well." We are told that Bartimaeus' vision was immediately restored, and he began to follow Jesus and the disciples.[34]

I am fascinated by many aspects of this story. This occurred in the early phase of Jesus' public ministry. Up until this point, no one had made a connection to who Jesus really was—that He may be the Messiah, the promised one sent to redeem the people of Israel. Yet, this blind beggar on the side of the road was the first to "see" this possibility when he referred to Jesus as "Son of David." Using this title, Bartimaeus directly correlated Jesus to the promise of God to King David that the Messiah would be born within his bloodline. Those closest to Jesus, this band of disciples, had not connected the dots as wisely as this simple man.

I am moved that Jesus showed compassion for the struggle of Bartimaeus' blindness. After being unable to see his family and friends for such a long time, imagine how he felt when Jesus spoke those healing words to him. After seeing nothing but darkness for so many years, it must have been a precious moment when the first thing Bartimaeus could finally see was the face of Jesus.

I first came to grasp on a personal level how profoundly God cares about our physical health when my husband received a shattering diagnosis of Acute Myeloid Leukemia. John was fifty-seven years old, and the epitome of stellar health. He could count on one hand the times he had ever missed work for being sick. At the time of his diagnosis, John regularly played tennis three times a week and was in extraordinary physical shape. He served as the managing partner of his accounting firm and was an active volunteer in causes near to his heart. His illness became an upheaval in our world. We both quickly experienced God's compassion for John and our situation. We began to rely upon the Lord for His concern and care regarding the details of the heavy burden of John's illness.

---

[34] Mark 10:46-52.

God Cares for Our Emotional Condition

Centuries ago, leprosy blighted many towns. The infectious disease caused severe, disfiguring skin sores and nerve damage. Anyone who caught leprosy was banished from the interior of their city and forced to live on the outskirts with other lepers in a colony to prevent the spread of this debilitating illness. Lepers were viewed as "unclean" by society and even by the leaders of the synagogue. The belief was that if you touched someone with leprosy, you too would be considered unclean, and you were prohibited to enter the temple to worship or offer sacrifices.

On his first preaching tour in Galilee, Jesus travelled village to village. One day on the outskirts of a new town, He neared a leper colony.

> *"A man with leprosy came and knelt in front of Jesus, begging to be healed. 'If you are willing, you can heal me and make me clean,' he said. Moved with compassion, Jesus reached out and touched him. 'I am willing,' he said. 'Be healed!' Instantly, the leprosy disappeared, and the man was healed."*[35]

This is a poignant story in Mark's gospel. Jesus encountered a man who had known the pain of loneliness. He desired human contact with anyone outside his leper colony. I find it fascinating that the leper never doubted that Jesus could heal him—his primary concern was whether or not Jesus wanted to heal him. This breaks my heart. I can relate to this leper. Can you?

During the first six months of John's struggle with leukemia, I stayed with him at the cancer hospital 24/7, trying to get what little sleep I could on a small, couch-like chair. I wanted to be with John, but my mother was also suffering with Alzheimer's. Up until his diagnosis, I had served as the primary caregiver for her. Once John became ill, I felt constantly pulled in two directions. I wanted

---

[35] Mark 1:40-42, The Living Bible.

to be there for him one hundred percent, but I tried to check on my mother as often as I could. My stomach was always in knots, and my heart was constantly anguished. I felt pulled in two different directions.

I can honestly say I never once doubted the ability of God. I knew He had the power to heal John and halt the speed of my mother's illness. Sitting up late at night watching John battle with pain, my mind wandered. I thought, Did God want to heal John? And if not, why? What reason could he have not to heal him? I believe this is how the leper must have felt.

When he chose to heal this leper, Jesus reached out and did something remarkable: he touched him. Jesus had compassion for the man. I am convinced that Jesus knew how long it had been since the leper had felt the simple joy of human touch. The leper had been scorned and labeled unclean for so long. He finally met someone who cared more about him than his disease. Jesus brought not only physical healing, but emotional healing as well. He made the leper feel whole again.

God Cares About Our Spiritual Wellness

In the village of Bethany, Jesus was blessed to be close friends with a group of siblings who lived together—Mary, Martha, and Lazarus. Their village was near the larger cities of Jericho and Jerusalem, and Jesus visited them whenever he was near. One day while visiting with them in their home, Martha was busy in the kitchen, working to prepare and serve a meal to Jesus. I can imagine pots clanging and tablecloths being shaken in the wind. I can see Martha with beads of sweat at her temples. While all this fussing took place, her sister Mary sat relaxed at the feet of Jesus, listening intently to him teach.

Seeing Mary sitting comfortably in the living room, Martha was clearly annoyed. She complained to Jesus saying, "Lord, do you not care that my sister has left me to serve alone? Tell her then to help me." I chuckle at this part of the story because I do not think Martha received the response she hoped to get from Jesus. He answered, "Martha, you are anxious and troubled about many things; one thing is needful. Mary has chosen the good portion, which shall not be taken away from her."[36]

This story has amused and infuriated many Christian women through the centuries, especially those considered to have "Type A" personalities. Many like to defend Martha and proclaim, "Well, someone had to pull a meal together. Who else was going to do the work? Mary should have gotten up and helped poor Martha." Despite the practicalities of this perspective, that was not the point Jesus wanted to drive home.

His foremost concern was for Martha's spiritual attitude and priorities. Jesus knew he would not be on Earth forever—and certainly not in this home. His visits were somewhat fleeting. He wanted to emphasize to Martha that when we are in the presence of God, we need to soak up every moment of His nearness and glean every morsel of His teaching.

How many times are we in the middle of an experience that we should recognize as exceptional, but we are distracted, and then we miss out on the beauty of the moment? Far too many for me to count. Because of my pressing agenda, I cease to see the sacred. I do not sense God's nearness. I do not gain His insight. When I reflect upon these missed opportunities, I am sad. I know God has forgiven me, so it is not the guilt of wrongdoing that weighs on me. Rather, I mourn the loss of moments that could have inspired me, occasions that could have spurred me to grow in my faith.

God cares about our spiritual health. He wants to fill us up with spiritual truths. God wants to plant seeds of new ideas within us about how we can make a difference and encourage us to strive for much-needed change in the world. His spirit wants to lead us in new ways to reach out and relieve the pain and suffering of others. God longs for our spirits to be joined with His in sweet

---

[36] Luke 10:38-42.

communion. I pray for God to remind me to keep my focus more aligned with His divine timing. I don't want to miss holy moments. I want to be aware of the sacred opportunities that cross my path when they arrive.

God Cares About Our Fears

One of the most repeated phrases in all of scripture is, "Do not be afraid." Both the Old and New Testaments are filled with these words spoken by God, as well as by prophets, angels, and apostles, reminding the children of God to let go of their fears.

Jesus spent a lot of time on the water. He and his disciples regularly went fishing to catch dinner. They often traveled by boat to reach towns and villages. One day, Jesus set out with His disciples on the Sea of Galilee. The sky was lovely, filled with bright sun. As the disciples cast their nets, Jesus settled down to take a nap. The Sea of Galilee was known for abrupt weather changes, and not long afterward, a vicious storm arose. Great winds tossed the boat, and waves crashed over the sides. The disciples grew afraid. They watched Jesus sleep soundly as they raced around bailing water, beginning to panic. Finally, a few of them went to wake Jesus saying, "Save us, Lord, we are perishing!" Jesus rose and rebuked the winds and the sea, and the storm silenced. The sea became calm and placid.[37]

Imagine the faces of the disciples as they dropped their buckets on the deck and stared at the sea. They looked up at the sky to see the dark clouds disappear and felt the warmth of the sun as it shone brightly once again. I imagine they were overcome with relief. The fact that Jesus did not take their cries for help lightly must have meant the world to them. To the contrary, he cared about their fears and acted swiftly to bring them out of harm's way. He gave them peace of mind in the midst of their turmoil.

---

[37] Matthew 8:23-27.

The opposite of fear is trust. If we can take our fears and give them to God, He will take them and dispel them on our behalf. He will, in turn, give us more faith to trust Him. If we keep our focus on the Lord, we can turn our attention away from the worries and concerns that fuel our fear. We can look to the one who has the power and wisdom to guide and direct us to overcome life's obstacles.

What does God want you to know about Him? That He cares about His children. God wants you to trust Him. He wants to love and care for you through the many seasons and trials of life. It is a joy to be His child.

Questions for Reflection

* Have you ever had a situation where you experienced God's concern and care regarding the physical health of you or a loved one? What difference did it make?

* The author shared a story about how Jesus healed a leper who confronts Him, saying, "If you are willing, you can heal me." Have you ever wondered if God desires to work in your life? Do you believe the Bible supports the idea that He does?

* Do you pray about your spiritual wellness? What do you believe God would like you to do to improve your spiritual life?

* The author shared that the most repeated phrase in all of Scripture is "Do not be afraid." Why do you believe fear can be so crippling in our quest to experience God's care for us as His child?

CHAPTER FIVE

"I Am Always with You"

The first four words in The Bible are "In the beginning, God..."[38] This simple phrase contains so much meaning. Let's unpack it a bit. It teaches us a profound truth: that God has always existed. We wonder, "How can that be? Isn't there a starting point for the existence of everything and everyone?" But God, the creator of the universe, had no beginning. The Bible also teaches that God will have no end. He is eternal in the truest sense of the word. In a psalm of Moses, he declares, "Lord, you have been our dwelling place throughout all generations. Before the mountains were born, or you brought forth the earth and the world, from everlasting to everlasting, you are God."[39]

Yahweh, the Hebrew name for God, means, "He who brings into existence whatever has been made." As the divine creator, the God of the Hebrews was unlike the pagan gods. He did not create humans and then toss them into the wind. He bound himself to His creation.

Centuries before the New Testament era, the prophet Isaiah predicted the

---
[38] Genesis 1:1.
[39] Psalm 90:1-2, NIV.

coming of the messiah to the nation of Israel. Isaiah proclaimed the Messiah would fulfill many roles, naming him "Wonderful Counselor, Mighty God, Everlasting Father, Prince of Peace."[40] All of these expectations required God's continuous presence in the world. How? He sent the Holy Spirit to serve as our Counselor. God's mighty power brought forth the incarnation. He remains our Everlasting Father because He has no beginning, and no end. Jesus became the Prince of Peace as he brought spiritual redemption to the world.

Six hundred years later, Jesus fulfilled Isaiah's prophesy. Jesus was born to Mary, who conceived him while a virgin engaged to Joseph, who became his earthly father. Joseph was visited in a dream by an angel of the Lord who reassured him that the baby Mary was carrying was conceived by the Holy Spirit. As Matthew recalls this event in his gospel, he quotes Isaiah from centuries earlier, "All this took place to fulfill what the Lord had spoken by the prophet, 'Behold, a virgin shall conceive and bear a son, and his name shall be called Emmanuel,' which means God with us."[41]

Emmanuel. God with us. What a powerful, comforting title to bestow upon Jesus. One of my favorite pieces of jewelry is a necklace, crafted in silver and gold, etched with the word "Emmanuel" on a small medallion. I love to wear it because it reminds me that wherever I go, I am not alone—God is always with me.

The incarnation was the act of God, who was in spirit form, being made into human form, in flesh and blood, in the person of Jesus Christ. We celebrate this miraculous occurrence in the Christian church during the holy season of Advent and Christmas. The disciple John wrote about this mystery of the incarnation in his gospel:

"And the Word became flesh and dwelt among us, full of grace and truth; we have beheld His glory, glory as of the only son from

---

[40] Isaiah 9:6.
[41] Matthew 1:22-23.

the Father...No one has ever seen God, the only son, who is in the bosom of the Father, He has made Him known."[42]

Why does it matter that God became flesh? For the people of this time in history, those who had the privilege to meet and follow Jesus were never the same again. Because Jesus came to the world, we have a Savior. Without God in the flesh, there would be no hope of eternal redemption for the living. God's choice to become human through the life of Jesus demonstrated His longing to reunite us and find a way to atone our sins.

The disciple Peter possessed an enthusiasm and zeal for Jesus that warms the heart. Despite his impetuous personality and sometimes impulsive tendencies, he seemed to have a natural gift of spiritual perception, as if looking through a spiritual lens and hearing with spiritual ears. Peter was in tune with God's presence and listened to His voice. After Jesus ascended back to Heaven following his resurrection, Peter labored faithfully as a missionary. Between his work among the Jews and the Apostle Paul's work among the Gentiles, the two disciples spread the gospel to the ends of the known world.

Sixty years after the resurrection, Peter wrote two letters to believers in the early church reminding them of the authenticity of their faith. He encouraged them not to fall prey to false teachers but to remember that their salvation was founded upon the man Jesus who lived a faithful life and died an atoning death. Although he was growing older, Peter wrote with heartfelt zeal when he shared, "For we did not follow cleverly devised myths when we made known to you the power and coming of our Lord Jesus Christ, but we were eyewitnesses of His majesty."[43] Peter counted among his greatest blessings in life the privilege to have personally known and followed Jesus. Being with Jesus meant everything to him. Time spent with God is our greatest investment in life.

---

[42] John 1:14; v18.
[43] II Peter 1:16.

Have you ever struggled with an overwhelming issue that you longed to share with a friend to gain their advice or insight? I have learned that it is often counterproductive to share such issues with a friend who cannot relate to my specific situation. It is wiser to choose someone who can understand what I have experienced and what I am feeling.

Fortunately for us, Jesus understands what it is like to be human. He experienced sadness, heartache, disappointment, and pain as he lived on Earth. He knows what it is like to be confused or frustrated. He knows how anger can build up inside us and then suddenly explode when we least expect it. Spending time with Jesus is so valuable for us. He genuinely understands and relates to what we are feeling when we share it with Him, "For we have not a high priest who is unable to sympathize with our weaknesses but one who in every respect has been tempted as we are, yet without sin."[44] We can pour our hearts out to Christ in prayer because He knows what it is like to struggle and to be tempted. He wants to listen and spend time hearing our concerns.

Becoming aware of God's presence is one of the greatest lessons we can learn as believers. We need to recognize the invisible spiritual senses within us to know that God is near and understand how He is always with us. I practice disciplines to help hone these senses. I regularly meditate upon God's word. I participate in individual and corporate worship. I sing to God to praise Him for His goodness and faithfulness. I keep a gratitude journal to chronicle the many ways I see God's hand in my life. All these activities build upon each other to heighten my spiritual awareness.

During the days when Jesus was arrested, tried, and crucified, the disciples were naturally afraid. Out of confusion, disappointment, and fear, most of them fled. I can't blame them. I know how hard it is to face your worst fear, especially after fighting so hard, for so long, to help the person you love.

But one remained. John stayed at the cross. He never left. He stood with

---

[44] Hebrews 4:15.

Jesus' mother, Mary, along with Mary Magdalene and a few others. That is the kind of friend you want when life falls apart. John knew that Jesus never turned his back on him, and so he chose to stay and be with his best friend while he was dying.

Following his death, Jesus' friends and family were devastated and heartbroken. Each grieved in their own way. I learned the hard lessons of grief in the loss of John. There is no clear path, no manual to follow. We must stumble through it to find our way through the darkness in the hope that we will one day see light in life again. Each of the followers of Jesus had a turning point which ultimately compelled them to move forward. My personal experience of grief led me closer to God, following a long period of questioning, restlessness, and disappointment. When I accepted that my doubts, fears, and anger would never drive God away nor cause Him to leave me, I had a breakthrough. The constancy of His presence and love are what sustained me in my darkest times. My feelings of grief were big, but we worship an even bigger God.

Mary Magdalene shared a significant relationship with Jesus. When they first met, Jesus cast out seven demons that traumatized and possessed her. He healed her emotionally and spiritually. He made her feel whole again. Imagine the joy and gratitude she felt after being set free of this evil trapped within her body for so many years. Once healed, Mary Magdalene became one of the most devout followers of Christ. She travelled with Jesus and his disciples, humbly providing for their daily needs, finding lodging, and preparing meals. There was nowhere else Mary would have been during the crucifixion—she stayed at the foot of the cross.

The day after the burial of Jesus, Mary Magdalene went to the tomb to grieve his death and be alone in the quiet of the morning. When she arrived, she noticed that the boulder that sealed the tomb had been rolled away. This naturally surprised and frightened her. She began to weep. Suddenly, two angels appeared. They asked her why she was crying, and Mary said, "Because they have taken away my Lord, and I do not know where they have laid Him."[45] Mary's spirit was already broken. Seeing His tomb empty must have felt like a sword stabbing through her heart.

Mary turned and saw a man standing behind her. He asked her why she was crying and for whom she was looking. Assuming he was the cemetery gardener, she replied, "Sir, if you have carried him away, tell me where you have laid him, and I will take him away." Just then, the man looked into her eyes and said perhaps the most beautiful word she had ever heard: "Mary." The moment He called her name, she knew it was Jesus, her precious Lord. She fell to her feet, reached out to Him, and said, "Teacher."

Jesus cautioned her, "Do not hold me, for I have not yet ascended to the Father, but go to my brethren and say to them, I am ascending to my Father and your Father, to my God and your God." Mary left to find the disciples to share the good news, proclaiming, "I have seen the Lord!"[46]

We will never know the unique condition of Jesus' body while at the tomb in this story from John's gospel. Jesus must have appeared noticeably different, or Mary would have recognized him. The text makes it seem that Jesus was in a transitional state during the process of ascending His spirit back to the Father. Nevertheless, we can learn volumes from how attuned Mary was to her spiritual senses and how her heart quickened to the voice of God.

When God calls our name, we need to listen. We need to train ourselves to hear Him by developing our spiritual intuition. I believe Jesus' injunction not to touch Him was His way of gently conveying that Mary would soon have to learn how to recognize Him without seeing Him with her eyes. She would have to sense His presence in other ways. This same instruction applies to us! We have not lived during an age when Jesus is physically present on earth, but we have many ways to sense His presence and feel His nearness in our lives. Remember—He is Emmanuel. He is God, always with us.

---

[45] John 20:13.
[46] John 20:15-17.

Developing my spiritual intuition requires devotion. Taking time away from my normal routine helps expand my horizons. A change of scenery really helps. Discovering a new space leads me to think more expansively about God. I create more "mind space" so that I may entertain broader and bigger ideas about Him. This fosters a spirit of expectation—willfully looking for God to act in my life. I look for new ways to experience His presence in unexpected places.

There was a time when this became critical for my emotional and spiritual survival. In the first couple of weeks spent at the hospital during John's cancer treatment, the days began to seem endless. Hours that used to speed by for me in my busy career at a bustling law firm seemed to drag on forever. I was desperately trying to connect with God and seek His wisdom about our dire situation, but it was difficult as I looked at the same four walls of a hospital room. We were in a funk.

As one of six children, John was close to all his siblings, and he was especially close to his brother Carl Jr., who he shared a room with growing up. At the time when John was hospitalized, Carl was a busy pastor, with a large church and many responsibilities, in a city two hours away from where we lived. He called John frequently to check in and cheer him up. After Carl made his first trip to visit John in the hospital, I believe he sensed that the two of us were emotionally drowning. He noticed that John was discouraged and frustrated, and that I was exhausted and barely holding on.

Being a man of great conviction and action, my beloved brother-in-law Carl approached the leadership of his church and informed them that from that point on, he would be taking every Friday off work to visit his brother in the hospital two hours away. Thus began a special experience that John and I both began to look forward to—Carl and his "Fun Fridays." The mornings always began by Carl bringing doughnuts and coffee, and after a brief visit with me, he promptly kicked me out of the hospital to give me the day off—then he and John began their special day together. I spent my time in various ways each week—walking in a nearby park, meeting a friend for lunch, or sitting alone in a quiet place. Carl's gift of time was exactly what John and I needed to expand the spiritual space in our minds and hearts. It became a lifeline for me when I was desperate to sense God's presence. It sustained us both over the course of many months. It refreshed John's spirit and reminded him that we were not alone in our bleak situation. We both knew that God was there with us.

In addition to the resurrection of Jesus, the arrival of the Holy Spirit was another monumental time in the history of our Christian faith. This occurred during the Jewish festival of Pentecost, and it is one of the great celebrations in the church. In secular culture, it is not nearly as well-known as Christmas or Easter, but for Christians, Pentecost is profoundly significant. Pentecost marks the giving of the Holy Spirit to the disciples and other believers as they met in Jerusalem per the instruction of Jesus, right before He left Earth for his second and final ascent to Heaven. This dramatic gathering transformed these confused, frightened individuals into men and women who would face martyrdom for what they believed. Pentecost was the birth of the church of Jesus Christ.

The gift of the Holy Spirit is essential to believers. Because of this gift, God now works with and through each one of us. In the Old Testament we saw how God worked collectively with His people, the nation of Israel. Now, with the advent of the Holy Spirit, God dwells within each of us. He is closer to us than we are to ourselves. It is the Spirit who enables us to see everything else in a new light.

Because the Holy Spirit is part of the trinity, in unity and constant communion with God the Father and Jesus the Son, He comforts and counsels us, and teaches us truth. The Spirit prays for us and speaks to us when needed. His inner presence is one of the greatest gifts we know as children of God.

What does God want you to know about Him? That He is always with you. You are never alone. His Holy Spirit is as close as your beating heart. What better way to go through life?

Questions for Reflection

* In what ways can you try to hone your "invisible spiritual senses" to become more aware of God's presence alongside you?

* How does thinking of Jesus as "Emmanuel" make a difference in your life?

* The author states that "The Holy Spirit is essential to believers." Describe the ways you recognize the Spirit's presence and work in your life.

* How do you know that God is always with you?

CHAPTER SIX

"Lean on Me"

When I think about the various injuries and surgeries the members of our family have endured, I realize how many times we were glad we kept crutches in the attic. I have had surgeries on my foot and my knee, and my son Mark broke his ankle in three places during his football years in high school. Crutches helped us navigate getting around while our bones healed. But, with a two-story home, we depended more heavily on another person to help us, even more than the crutches, to go up and down the stairs. The crutches were too wobbly; they felt dangerous. Having someone to lean on is what supported us and enabled us to navigate the obstacle safely.

I have always loved the old song "Lean on Me" by Bill Withers. This charming song describes the dependability of a friend by being able to lean on them for support and encouragement.

My friend Patti has been a steadfast friend for over forty years. We met in college and shared the process of growing from teenagers into young adults. When we look back together, we remember many times where one of us made unwise choices. Somehow, though, we were fortunate that we rarely made regrettable decisions simultaneously. One of us was always there for the other to lean on. God continues to use Patti in my life in many ways. When we go too long without talking, I start to sense a strong desire for a "Patti fix." After investing in each other's lives for over four decades, we continue to lean on one another for much-needed wisdom, making tough decisions, and surviving the trials and tragedies life brings. Patti has taught me that if you are going to lean on someone to get you through your struggles, you need to be confident of their loyalty and love.

As we grow in our faith, God wants us to lean on Him. The mark of a mature Christian is often evidenced by how one has learned to do this through the years. Whether it is to receive daily inspiration or endure seasons of great difficulty, a wise believer knows that God is always there for them. He is honored when we choose to lean on Him regularly.

One of the reasons we can confidently lean on the Lord is because of His unending love for us. He never grows weary of hearing us call out His name. The Psalmist captures this beautifully, "I have trusted in Thy steadfast love; my heart shall rejoice in Thy salvation."[47] His love never changes, and He is not fickle. God's love for us has existed since the beginning of time. It never diminishes. His love continues to grow through the ages.

A great morsel of truth is that as we grow in our faith, the more we learn to lean on God, and the easier it becomes. We each share a unique history with Him. When I face a barricade that seems unyielding, I simply reflect upon other obstacles that earlier rose in my path. I remember when God helped me face those hardships and gave me the wherewithal to overcome. When I am confronted by someone who intends to harm me, I recall the occasions when God rescued me from others within a host of awkward, difficult situations. Remembering how God delivered me before gives me the courage to lean on Him again.

---

[47] Psalm 13:5.

A strong example of someone who built a great history with God is the life of King David. When he was young, he shepherded his family's herd of sheep. Some nights, David had to confront serious dangers. God heard his cries, and He always answered. When a lion appeared and threatened to attack the sheep, and possibly attack David along with the flock, God gave him the strength to slay the beast. The same thing occurred when a bear carried away a lamb. Again, God was there for him, giving David the strength to slay the bear and save the lamb. He empowered David with courage to meet the crisis. This shepherd boy learned from an early age that he could lean on God—even in the most fearful circumstances. I believe this was one of the many secrets to David's great faith.

When David was a teenager and prepared to fight the mighty giant Goliath, King Saul wondered if he was too young for the battle. When the king questioned David, he quickly replied, "The Lord who delivered me from the paw of the lion and from the paw of the bear will deliver me from the hand of this Philistine."[48] We need to reflect on the times when God was there for us. In addition, we should never forget the times God used others to be there for us when we needed someone in the flesh to lean on.

My friend Andrew is a gifted, albeit amateur, artist. We met in college and together experienced some of the craziest predicaments I've ever been in. He makes me laugh harder than anyone. Andrew used to do something that brought me much joy. Following our more colorful escapades, he would draw a picture that perfectly captured the moment of calamity I had engaged in and then give it to me. I remember hanging those drawings up in my room to serve as reminders that Andrew and I always had each other's back. It was great to know we could lean on one another and come to each other's rescue when needed.

Healthy spiritual habits develop when believers trust God over and over. Behavior specialists differ over how long it takes to establish a new habit; however, they agree that daily practicing the intended new activity greatly

---

[48] I Samuel 17:37.

increases the likelihood it will become a perpetual behavior.

Reading the Bible and praying every day are wonderful ways to incorporate important spiritual disciplines into our lifestyle. Start small—decide to read one verse or passage each day and spend five minutes in prayer. Over time, your hunger to know more of God's truth and sense His presence will eventually kick in. And then, you will be hooked! You will desire to tackle whole chapters at a time, and before you know it, you may just commit to read an entire book of The Bible.

You may consider increasing your prayer life by spending time with the Lord multiple times throughout your day. You may enjoy meditating—sitting quietly just to listen to God. The more you seek to soak up His presence, the easier it becomes to lean on Him.

Depending upon God helps eradicate our fears. This is a powerful way to live. The prophet Isaiah shared, "Behold, God is my salvation; I will trust and not be afraid."[49] Too often in life, we allow fear to trip us up and prevent us from doing what we know is best. Sometimes fear can paralyze us, and it blocks the way for wholesome relationships with other people. Fear can block us from moving forward and growing in our faith. Trusting God is the opposite of fear.

I have found that people who lean on the Lord seem to be happier than others. King Solomon wrote, "Happy is he who trusts in the Lord."[50] When we release our problems and concerns and hand them over to God, we can lean on Him to guide us. He will provide us with His strength and wisdom. We will discover a deep satisfaction within. We will lead a happier life.

In the gospels, Jesus called us to become salt and light to the world.[51] Salt adds flavor to food, and it helps to preserve meat. As Christians, we can be like salt as we bring a zest to life and help preserve the truth of God's Word. Light

---

[49] Isaiah 12:2a.
[50] Proverbs 16:20b.
[51] Matthew 5:13-15.

exposes darkness and shows us the way on our path. As we seek to be light in the world, we can shine God's light upon others as we model the joy that a healthy relationship with God can bring. We can share the gospel with people to shine God's truth into their lives.

As we lean on the Lord, others will notice that God is making a positive difference in our life. Sometimes our actions speak louder than our words. The book of Proverbs explains, "He put a new song in my mouth, a song of praise to our God. Many will see and put their trust in the Lord."[52] It is amazing how contagious a joy-filled, trusting believer can be to someone who longs to know God. When nonbelievers see Christians leaning on the Lord, it may encourage them. Our example can give someone the courage they need to take a leap of faith to get to know and trust God.

Derek Anthony Redmond is a retired British runner. During his career, he held the British record for the 400-meter sprint. He won gold medals at both the World Championships and European Championships. In 1992, he fulfilled his dream of becoming an Olympic athlete, and he travelled to Barcelona to represent his country. The moment he heard the gun, Derek began to run his heart out. He maintained a steady lead, and he ran with full force, as fast as his legs could carry him. When he reached the halfway mark, a sharp pain shot up his leg, and he collapsed. His hopes were dashed. As all the other runners passed him, Derek writhed in pain with a ripped hamstring. As he heard the cheers of the crowd as other runners completed the race, Derek made a decision. He would not win, but he would finish. With tears streaming down his cheeks, he struggled to his feet and hobbled alone toward the finish line. He trudged along, taking step after painful step, determined to finish this race of a lifetime. Then, there was a small commotion in the crowd. An older, gray-haired man pushed his way down, jumped over the railing, and fought off the security guards to pass the officials. He made his way to Derek on the other side of the track. Derek's

---

[52] Proverbs 40:3.

father wrapped his arms around his son and spoke words of love to him. You could see the relief on Derek's face as he leaned on his father and strained to take each step. Together, they crossed the finish line.

We do not need to struggle alone. God wants us to lean on Him as our Heavenly Father, just as Derek leaned on his earthly father. We can run the race of life depending upon God for His supernatural strength and steadfastness. He will always be there for us, every step of the way. But sometimes, in His divine intervention, God provides the perfect person we need to lean on, at the right time, just as He sent Derek's father to him while he was limping on the track.

I have leaned on my cousin Pam through some of life's most heartbreaking moments. When I could not be with my mother as she was dying in a hospice house because I was with John at the cancer hospital, Pam stayed with my mother on my behalf. She was there, taking turns with my faithful friend Donna, to spend mother's last days with her. Pam was there at two in the morning when my mother took her last breath. It gives me great peace to know that to the very end Pam surrounded my mother with unending love.

I am bountifully blessed with sisters-in-law—Jane, Becky, Beth, Vairin, Kathryn, Wendy and Janet—who are bulwarks of strength. I leaned on them daily for their gifts of practical assistance, discernment and prayer while we were struggling with John's long illness. They became my "Dream Team." My friend Jett tirelessly coordinated hot meals for our family for a year during our crisis. Most people would have grown weary and stopped much sooner, yet Jett's devotion and love knew no timetable.

My dear friends Mark and Anne are the godparents of our children. Mark was John's best friend since childhood, and we named our second son Mark after him. Their presence in my life is like a drink of cold water to my parched spirit. I approach Mark often, seeking his counsel and advice, and he always offers guidance with patience, love and kindness. Anne understands me on a "soul level" and I lean on her for prayer support, wisdom, and encouragement.

Her "mailbox dusters" are some of my fondest treasures—notes, photos, quotes and more. Sometimes you can lean on individuals from many miles away.

My friend Nancy repeatedly drops everything at a moment's notice to be by my side when I need her. She handles difficult details on my behalf when I am at my wit's end. My friends Lori and Karen have seen me at my worst, yet they both continue to bolster me with humor, positive spirits and much-needed perspective. My friend Peggy is my devoted walking buddy. A wise soul and keen listener, Peggy's faith is contagious, and her heart is pure. My friend Diane continues to text and call me just to "check in," a loving reminder that although I am a widow and live alone, I am surrounded by many who care for me. Lynda is my maverick, beer-drinking buddy whose enthusiasm and voracious creativity constantly inspires and fuels me. My friend Rosemary's calming presence reassures me and gives me hope.

What does it take to become a person who others want to lean on? God can use us in big and small ways to be there for others. To become a person who others want to lean on may require being somewhere that is hard to be, speaking words someone needs to hear, conducting research to help solve a problem, making someone laugh when they need it most, responding on a moment's notice, providing help for as long as it takes, and never giving up on someone you love. God places people in our lives to help us lean on them, and He uses us to do the same in return. I have learned that leaning on God involves allowing yourself to lean on others whom He gently places in your path.

What does God want you to know about Him? He wants you to lean on Him. There is no better way to feel safe or more secure than when you are being held up by His loving arms.

Questions for Reflection

* The author shares "As we grow in our faith, the more we learn to lean on God, the easier it becomes." Do you agree? Why or why not?

* How did the Biblical stories of David shared in this chapter speak to you?

* Would others consider you a person they can lean on in life? Why or why not?

* Who in your life has been a strong person to lean on in difficult times? Do you believe they were used by God in your life?

CHAPTER SEVEN

"My Mercies are New Every Morning"

One of my favorite times of day is when I first wake up but before I get out of bed. It is a special "in between" time when I am making the transition from blissful sleep to the recognition that a new day has dawned. As I open my eyes, still clinging to my pillow, I take time to pause and reflect before the day officially begins. In these quiet moments, I am keenly aware of both my gratitude and anticipation. My spirit is grateful that God brought me through the night with rejuvenating rest. My heart anticipates a fresh new day. There are no blunders and no regrets. The mistakes of yesterday are gone.

Likewise, New Year's Day is a reflective holiday for me. I welcome the chance to look back on the past year, taking stock of the highs and lows, celebrations and regrets. I like to explore how I have grown in my faith or if I experienced any blockages preventing spiritual growth. It is a time to lay it all out before God. I thank God for His presence and involvement in my life, and I ask Him for strength and forgiveness to overcome the areas where I have yet to make progress.

One of my children usually gives me a new calendar for Christmas. Over the New Year's holiday, I love flipping through the pages, viewing the pristine squares, with no marks nor scribbles. The empty spaces gleam back at me, ready to begin a new year with a clean slate. What a glorious gift from God!

Despite our fervent devotion to the Lord and genuine desire to please Him, we still stumble and fall, making mistakes every day that we grow to regret. Why is this? This has been a question for all generations throughout history. The only answer that makes sense to me is that we still possess a natural inclination toward sin. Each time I choose what is right and best in God's eyes, I have made that choice by turning my back on what is wrong.

As we mature in our faith, choosing what is right in certain facets of our life becomes easier. We no longer need to weigh each specific choice with the painstaking effort required in our youth. Rather, we simply act upon habit for what we have learned is the highest and best way. I like to call this "hard-won wisdom."

Despite the progress great or small that we make in our spiritual walk, there will always be times in our lives where the choices will not be crystal clear. We will need to think carefully through our options and seriously weigh the consequences of our decisions. Sometimes we will choose what is right. Other times we will choose what is weak or cowardly. Sometimes we choose what appears to be the easy way out. It is during these times that we often disappoint God.

The sins that continue to trip me up are different than those that affect you. What you struggled with for years and have now conquered might be the very sins which I am currently battling. We all need God's grace and mercy because we will never achieve perfection or stand blameless while living in the here and now.

Fortunately for us, we worship who I like to call "The God of Second Chances." His grace and mercy flow freely into our lives. To understand and appreciate these two gifts from God, I believe it is important to distinguish the difference between them.

Grace is God giving us something we do not deserve, something which we cannot and have not earned. The New Testament emphasizes the concept of grace as the foundation of our salvation, "All have sinned and fall short of the glory of God. We are justified by His grace as a gift, through the redemption which is in Christ Jesus."[53] Of all the incredible miracles in both the Old and New Testaments, I firmly believe that the greatest one of all is God's grace. He chose to allow the blood of Jesus to be shed at Calvary to atone for the sins of humanity. It is a pure gift, completely undeserved by us, yet given willingly to us straight from the heart of God.

Sometimes God's grace is so overwhelming that people simply cannot contain it. They want to earn God's grace; they want to earn their salvation. Some segments of Christianity emphasize legalism. This is an approach to faith which insists on strict adherence to God's laws, such that it seems like one must earn their salvation by doing good deeds and never caving to the temptation of sin. But God does not work on a point system. He does not dole out salvation to those who follow more rules and regulations than others. When we make faultlessness our primary aim, we have missed the whole point of God's grace.

Whereas grace is God giving us something we do not deserve, mercy is when God withholds punishment we do deserve because of the sins we have committed. Mercy demonstrates God restraining from action, whereas grace shows God taking action.

We learn in Paul's letter to the church in Rome that, "The wages of sin is death."[54] We are all guilty according to God's holy law. Since the payment for sin is death, we all deserve to receive eternal death because we have all sinned. But in His mercy, God pardons us and does not permit the punishment we fully deserve.

---

[53] Romans 3:23.
[54] Romans 6:23.

The gospel of Christ is topsy turvy, simply upside down. We don't get what we do deserve, yet we do get what we cannot earn. We deserve death, but we get life. We cannot earn eternal life because it is free. The mercy and grace of God work together to produce the wonder of salvation.

Centuries ago, when the Israelites were mourning the destruction of their beloved city of Jerusalem, along with their glorious temple, the prophet Jeremiah spoke to them:

> *"But this I call to mind, and therefore I have hope: the steadfast love of the Lord never ceases, His mercies never come to an end; they are new every morning; Great is thy faithfulness. The Lord is my portion, therefore I will Hope in Him."*[55]

God's mercy has a ripple effect, causing much to happen in our lives. We are never the same again because of this loving gift that God bestows upon us in full measure each day.

God's Mercies Cleanse Us

Sin erects a wall that disrupts the fellowship we enjoy with God. The disciple John put it aptly, "God is light and in Him is no darkness at all."[56] As believers, we receive forgiveness for all our past, present, and future sins when we accept Christ as our Savior. But, as we continue to make poor choices, we are wise to repent and confess each day so that we will know the joy of having our sins wiped from our lives forever. "If we confess our sins, He is faithful and just, and will forgive our sins and cleanse us from all unrighteousness."[57] It is impossible to know fellowship with God when we stand before Him tainted with sin,

---

[55] Lamentations 3:22-24.
[56] I John 1:5.
[57] I John 1:9.

in the radiant light of His righteousness. Thus, I confess and ask forgiveness throughout my day because I do not want any time to lapse when I could be enjoying sweet fellowship with the Lord.

The prophet Isaiah employs a vivid metaphor to describe this cleansing: "Though your sins are like scarlet, they shall be as white as snow."[58] There is nothing as pure and clean as freshly fallen snow. This is how God sees us once we have been cleansed of the sin in our lives. We stand before Him in purity and holiness. God's fellowship is worth everything. His abiding presence, hope, and love sustain me. The joy of His cleansing keeps me ever close to Him.

God's Mercies Humble Us

Sometimes when I ponder God's plentiful mercies, I am in awe of the countless times He has forgiven me over and over for the same sins. Doesn't He grow weary that I never seem to learn? But each time, God withholds the punishment I deserve and wipes my slate clean, offering forgiveness. He gives me hope for a new chance tomorrow to choose a higher way. I am humbled that He never gives up on me.

"How can you say to your brother, 'Let me take the speck out of your eye' when all the time there is a plank in your own eye? You hypocrite!"[59] Jesus comes down strongly on those who judge. How can I have the audacity to judge another person who annoys me with their repeated blunders? God's mercies humble me, and in doing so, I realize I need to keep my eyes focused on my own lane, overlooking the fault of others. I should count my blessings that God's mercies continue to cover my annoying, repeated mistakes. I have enough of my own issues to be concerned about without spending precious time or energy on the faults of others.

---

[58] Isaiah 1:18

[59] Matthew 7:4

God's Mercies Change Us

Despite my repeated failures, there are moments when God and I celebrate a victory over a long-fought sin that has been entrenched in my life. These times are precious to me as I journey through this life of faith. I wish these victories were far more frequent, but God, in His patience, is not finished with me yet. This ongoing process toward holiness is called "sanctification." In simple terms, it means we draw closer to "being made clean before God." This is how we grow in divine grace as we accept God's mercy and apply it to our lives.

"And we all, with unveiled face, beholding the glory of the Lord, are being changed into His likeness from one degree of glory to another; for this comes from the Lord who is the Spirit."[60] This is the treasure of our faith. God bestows liberty to live as free people, banishing the stronghold of sin's chains upon us. When we choose God and His light over sin and darkness, we begin to change, step by step, slowly becoming more like Jesus.

Have you recognized the face of Christ in another person? It is a beautiful sight. I recall many moments where I saw the love of Jesus in the face of my mother. She lived into her nineties. She weathered life's storms, and with God's help and strength, she lived each day with hope and contentment, despite her affliction with Alzheimer's. I saw His light in her face as she thanked her nurses and aides each time they did even the slightest task for her.

I saw the hope of Jesus in the face of a child living in an orphanage in Bolivia. As he was served hot meals each day by loving staff members, his face shined with certainty that he was a child of God. He knew that he no longer had to live in a park without a jacket to protect him from the wind and chill at night. God provides for him and gives him the security he needs each day.

I saw the peace of Jesus in the face of my precious father-in-law Carl, after losing my dear mother-in-law Monk, his soul mate of seventy-five years. Even though he felt a tremendous hole in his heart, he still woke up every

---

[60] II Corinthians 3:18.

day, grateful for the many good years he and Monk shared together. He looks forward in peace, knowing she is waiting on him in Heaven. What a glorious reunion awaits Carl.

God's Mercies Give Us Confidence

Cleansed, forgiven people tend to be more confident than others. They don't carry the heavy baggage of guilt that weighs them down and trips them up. They accept God's gift of mercy with glad hearts and live freely in the moment. Cleansed people do not fear the future for they know with certainty that God is in control and His mercies will continue to flow.

"Cleanse your hands, you sinners, and purify your hearts."[61] When our hands are clean and our hearts are pure, we are free to enjoy the refreshing presence of the Lord. We experience a confidence we never knew before. We can be bold and self-assured as we dispense His mercies and grace to others. We become like one beggar showing another where he has found food. The writer of Hebrews understood this well. "Let us then, with confidence, draw near to the throne of grace, that we may receive mercy and find grace to help in time of need."[62] Without fear or concern, God longs for us to approach Him and share our hearts.

What does God want you to know about Him? That His mercies are new every morning. Think about that each day before you get out of bed.

---

[61] James 4:8.
[62] Hebrews 4:16.

Questions for Reflection

* The author discusses the difference between grace and mercy. Describe your understanding of these two concepts. Have you seen them at work in your life?

* Have you ever caught yourself trying to earn God's grace? Why is this a futile attempt in a life of faith?

* How do you feel after confessing a sin and being forgiven by God?

* How does God's mercy give you confidence?

CHAPTER EIGHT

"I Welcome Repentant Hearts"

In the Old Testament, the relationship that God had with His people was very corporate in nature. God chose that phase of history to work with, and relate to, His people collectively rather than as individuals. As he was molding them into a spiritual nation, He brought laws, a moral code, and civil regulations to them to bring unity and instruction on how to lead upstanding lives. God desired that Israel become a blessing to all the other nations of the world.

During this time, God spoke to His people through judges, kings, priests, and prophets. These leaders occupied the highest roles in society. They were respected as the people's representatives of God. Priests played a significant role in the worship and sacrifices offered in the temple. The Hebrews knew the history of Adam and Eve, and they understood how original sin in the Garden of Eden created an enduring barrier in humanity's relationship with God. His people grasped that humankind inherited this propensity to sin and, along with it, they began an ongoing struggle that prevented harmony with God.

Following the original sin committed by the first man and woman, I find it interesting that one of the first actions they took was to sew loincloths to cover their shame before God. This act is interpreted by theologians as history's first offering. This step on the part of the first couple was an effort to cover or atone for their sin and restore the fellowship they had enjoyed with God.

Hebrew people continued the tradition of making offerings to God to symbolically atone for sin for centuries. Individuals were obligated because of perpetual sin to make a sacrifice in the sanctuary by the High Priest once a year in the Holiest of Holies. This was a sacred place in the temple reserved for this special day of atonement. Each person was required to provide a substitute life in place of their own. Tradition held that individuals must choose an animal, for the law stated that blood had to be shed. God honored the choice of the purest animal, the most unblemished one owned. This symbolized the necessity of man to present himself as perfect and without sin before God. Therefore, once a year, the people brought their best lamb to the temple to serve as a sacrifice for the high priest to slaughter to atone for their sin.

Most important, God mandated that sacrifices be made by individuals with an honest, repentant heart. People must genuinely desire to be forgiven and made clean by God in order to receive His forgiveness. The Psalmist understood this well, "The sacrifice acceptable to God is a broken spirit; a broken and contrite heart, O God, thou will not despise."[63] Going through the motions of making an offering to God without authentic repentance rings hollow in the ears of the Lord.

The original Hebrew word which we translate in English as "repentance" is "teshuva." It is more accurately translated and understood as "a turning."[64] The

---

[63] Psalm 51:17.

[64] Strong, James. *The New Strong's Guide to Bible Words: An English Index to Hebrew and Greek Words*, Nashville, TN: Thomas Nelson Inc., 2008.

root word of this verb occurs nearly a thousand times in Scripture. In spiritual terms, teshuva means turning away from disobedience and evil and turning toward God and His goodness.

This helps me to more fully understand repentance. When I recognize my sins, it stirs regret and anguish within me. Why? Because I know that my choices and attitudes have gone against God and His ways. My thoughts and actions have hurt Him and other people. My heart mourns how my sin has broken the communion I enjoy with God. This strong sense of remorse propels me to turn my back upon my sin and turn my face toward God.

If done in earnest, this spiritual turning can fundamentally change a person's relationship with God. When you experience authentic repentance, all manner of beliefs and habits can change with it. Your thinking becomes new, and you choose to focus on more positive, life-affirming thoughts that please God. This often leads to a change of heart—you no longer desire the short-term, false sense of security that your sinful activities used to bring. Rather, you endeavor to invite God's light into your life. You enjoy new knowledge of God's truth and seek to remain in His presence. Your actions and activities become new.

A friend of mine in college struggled with habitual lying. She was a Christian, and her entanglement in this sin weighed her down. She lied more to cover previous falsehoods. She fabricated stories to professors to get out of class assignments; she concocted stories to protect her reputation. After a while, she could not remember all the untruths she had conjured. The consequences of her sinful behavior became serious. She grew tired of living a life of deception. At last, she decided to repent before God and make a 180-degree turn, choosing to tell the truth from that point on. Years later, she reflected that the experience of repentance brought her a new life of freedom. Living in truth helped her draw closer to the Lord and restored many broken relationships with others. This demonstrates the transformative power of turning away from sin and turning toward God's goodness and light.

In the mid-1600s, a group of English and Scottish theologians, known as the Westminster Assembly, met over a two-year period to craft a catechism, a comprehensive document used to teach the Christian faith to children and new adult converts. This document became known as the Westminster Catechism. It was written in a question-and-answer format and included 107 questions designed to teach the components of the Reformed Christian faith. Many Protestant churches no longer employ the Westminster Catechism; perhaps they have developed more high-tech or engaging ways to appeal to a contemporary audience. Nonetheless, I still love the succinct manner and deep truths the Catechism reveals.

My favorite question in the Catechism is its very first one. Many children of my generation raised in a reformed faith tradition will forever remember this profound truth:

Q: What is the chief end of man?

A: Man's chief end is to glorify God and to enjoy Him forever.[65]

What a lovely way to look at the purpose and meaning of all of life. This one statement explains why we are here, why God created the world, and why we long to have a relationship with Him. It is so simple: we are here to glorify God and to enjoy Him forever. Repentance is so incredibly necessary in our faith. When rebellion takes over our life, we must make the effort to rekindle our fellowship with God.

Turning away from sin and turning our heart toward God is the key to restoration. Returning to the place where we bask in God's presence brings peace and delight to the soul. It makes life worth living. God is pleased to accept our heartfelt repentance and our heart's desire to change.

The many offerings and sacrifices in the Old Testament paved the way for Jesus to come to Earth. As the promised Messiah, Jesus came to redeem God's people and the world. While living as a human being for thirty-three years, Je-

---

[65] The Westminster Shorter Catechism, Unabridged Start Publishing LLC, November 2012.

sus led a sinless life, so that He could be a pure, unblemished sacrifice for all of humanity.

As Paul proclaims in Romans, "All have sinned and fall short of the glory of God."[66] No one is exempt. We are all sinners. According to the Levitical law of the Israelites which required animal sacrifices at the temple, the shedding of blood in death was necessary to atone for sin. The book of Hebrews explains, "Without the shedding of blood, there is no forgiveness of sin."[67] God could not grant forgiveness without atonement. His holiness and righteousness could not be compromised. His perfection and pure character could not tolerate being in the presence of the darkness and wretchedness of sin. Something had to be done to cancel the debt of sin. An offering of blood had to be paid.

Because of His great love for us, God allowed Jesus to serve as a substitute for us. He accepted the precious, sacrificial blood of Christ on the cross of Calvary to pay the penalty of our sin. The Book of Hebrews summarizes beautifully what Jesus accomplished in this great offering:

> *"For Christ has entered not into a sanctuary made of hands to appear in the presence of God on our behalf. Nor was it to offer Himself repeatedly, as the High Priest enters the Holy Place yearly with blood not his own. Christ has appeared once for all to put away sin by the sacrifice of Himself."*[68]

In this selfless act, Jesus became the new lamb—his blood was the ultimate sacrifice to pay for all of humanity's debt to sin. While he was being crucified and hanging on the cross, I imagine that Jesus remembered the haunting words spoken to Him by his cousin John the Baptist, "Behold the lamb of God, who

---

[66] Romans 3:23.
[67] Hebrews 9:22.
[68] Hebrews 9:24-26, selected verses.

takes away the sin of the world."[69] Perhaps Jesus recalled images of people in long lines in front of the temple, trying to keep their lambs still on their shoulders as they waited to present to the priest the best of their flock as a sacrifice.

The sins which Jesus died for were not His own. They were all the malicious, evil, hurtful thoughts, words, and deeds committed from the beginning of time. The sins Jesus died for were the missed opportunities to lift others up and help those in need. The blood Jesus shed was for the loving acts never performed to spread God's goodness. His body was given for all the moments we choose to remain silent rather than defend an innocent person or share encouraging words with the forlorn.

Before I partake in Holy Communion, I thank God that if I had been the only person in the whole world at the time, Jesus would have died just for me. His blood was freely given in love for the forgiveness of my sin and your sin. Our forgiveness cost him his life. Our salvation was bought with a precious price.

What does God want you to know about Him? That He welcomes repentant hearts. His love and grace respond in forgiveness, and our relationship is immediately restored. Fellowship with God is the sweetest you will ever know.

---

[69] John 1:29.

Questions for Reflection

* What does repentance mean to you? How has it played a role in your relationship with God?

* Why did the author believe that "Repentance is so incredibly necessary in our faith?"

* How does repentance relate to atonement?

* Why do you suppose that Jesus has been referred to as "the lamb of God?"

CHAPTER NINE

"I Keep My Promises"

When I ponder the glue that holds my significant relationships together, I realize how integral loyalty is to me. Friendships lacking this quality seem to easily fade. I find those who persist in staunch loyalty are the ones who, for me, remain lifelong friends. I prize loyalty because I am passionately loyal to those I love.

Loyalty came naturally to me growing up in a family that showed love to one another despite the downfalls, poor decisions, or idiotic tendencies we may have exhibited at times. I remember my two older brothers, Chuck and Rick, teasing me mercilessly when we were growing up. But if anyone else tried to tease me, they had to contend with the wrath of the Harvey boys. Loyalty to their sister was paramount.

More times than I like to admit, I lost my purse and the house keys along with it, or I ran out of gas in our rickety car. My sweet father always came to my rescue. He never lectured nor ridiculed me for my carelessness because he knew mistakes were part of life. He was fiercely loyal to me. My Dad knew that I did not intend to do stupid things, they just sometimes happened.

My mother demonstrated loyalty differently than my father. She was the one who kept me accountable to do what was right and best with others, often in complex, trying situations. I am sure it was challenging for her to be the voice of reason in my life, but it always sprung from her loyal heart. Her maternal protection was like a mama bear with her baby cub. She wanted to save me, yet instead taught me how to be strong and defend myself in tough situations.

I remember the moment when I knew for sure that I wanted to marry John. After dating for about six months, he confirmed that he would attend a business association's speech contest in which I was a finalist. He made the commitment to me a month before the event. As the evening drew closer, other obligations crept up in his schedule, and I knew they were probably more important. Part of me wanted to release him from his commitment, however, I knew it would mean a lot if he could be there to cheer me on. I wanted his calming presence to support me that night. John never wavered. He simply said, "I made a promise to you, Kim." That was it for me—I was smitten. He was a man of his word. His loyalty sustained thirty-three years of marriage before he lost a courageous battle with leukemia and went to be with the Lord.

My relationship with God is also all about loyalty. He is true to His word, and He always keeps His promises. From my earliest recollections in life, I cannot recall a moment when I did not know God—what a blessed way to grow up. Part of my identity is wrapped up in my certainty of His love for me. I am confident of His loyalty.

A promise is "a pledge to do something specific; to bring about, or to fully provide; to give ground for expectation that the act will be fulfilled." I love that last part: that a promise "gives ground for expectation." Perhaps that is why loyalty is so critical in our significant relationships. When a promise is made, we expect that it will be fulfilled. When it is not, we are disappointed and sometimes devastated. Our hopes are dashed, and our trust in the one who made the promise is broken to pieces.

How grateful I am that God always fulfills His promises. His ability to keep promises is woven throughout His character. God's loyalty and faithfulness guarantee that He will never disappoint. He will always fulfill what He pledges.

Years ago, a student in one of my Bible Studies approached me after class and asked me, "How do you approach building your life of faith?" What an insightful question. I paused and then replied, "I have built my life of faith by claiming and clinging to God's promises." The student was intrigued. She encouraged me to create a Bible study around this idea—so I did. In researching the concept, I found many apt portions of the Bible to explore. When I taught the study, we enjoyed many lively discussions about the promises of God that resonated in unique ways with each of us.

As a young woman, I built my marriage to John upon the vows we made to one another at the altar. Likewise, I chose to build my life upon God's promises to me and my pledge of commitment to Him.

God's promises impact our lives in many ways. Some of His promises are vast and overwhelming in scope, while others are personal and straightforward. However, all of them are promises we can count on to build a meaningful walk of faith to sustain us over a lifetime. I encourage you to read the Bible and discover the promises of God that resonate with you. Diligently plant them in your heart and mind. Claim His promises in prayer, and cling to them. Meditate on them. The ones I find particularly poignant, I write on notecards and post on my mirror. The promises of God can become your life's foundation—they will solidify your relationship with the Lord.

I will further share how I have done this in my life with the hope that it may provide a possible method to follow in your own life.

I like to think of my life as a circle. The foundation of my life is based upon God's promises in four distinct areas, represented as follows:

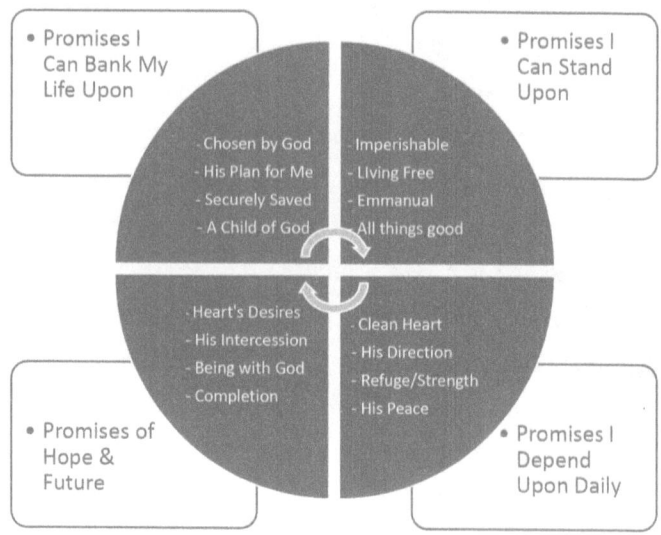

The reason I have chosen a circle to represent my life is because the shape is continuous, just like life. To understand how this works for me, I start at the top left and move clockwise, listing the specific promises I choose to claim and cling to, each one building upon the next, as I experience my life of faith. Each promise is found in God's Word, and I take Him at His word because He has proven through history and my own life that He can be trusted.

Promises I Can Bank My Life Upon

These are the absolute truths among God's promises that I choose as the "solid rocks" of my life's building blocks. I am willing to die for these truths. Without them, I am nothing, and life is not worth living. I encourage you to reflect upon your life. For what are you willing to die? This will help shape your convictions and chart your course. Here are the promises I can bank my life upon:

Chosen by God – Ephesians includes the promise, "He chose us in Him before the foundation of the world…He destined us in love to be His through

Jesus Christ."[70] My sense of self arises from this promise from God. Even before the world was created, God knew who I would be, and He chose me to know Him and be a part of His fold.

His Plan for Me – There is a beautiful benediction in the book of Hebrews that summarizes God's plan for my life:

"Now may the God of peace who brought again from the dead our Lord Jesus, the great shepherd of the sheep, by the blood of the eternal covenant, equip you with everything good that you may do His will, working in you that which is pleasing in His sight, through Jesus Christ; to whom be glory for ever and ever."[71]

God's plan is to equip me to do His will, which will make Him smile. Simply stated, that is my life's purpose.

Securely Saved – In Romans, Paul succinctly summarizes exactly what we need to do to receive God's gift of salvation. I love its simplicity. I can rely on this promise if doubts or temptation arise, for I know with every fiber of my being that my salvation is secure. Paul wrote, "If you confess with your lips that Jesus is Lord and believe in your heart that God raised Him from the dead, you will be saved."[72]

A Child of God – The epistle of I John holds me up and reminds me of my role in God's Kingdom: "See what love the Father has given us that we should be called children of God."[73] One of the greatest privileges is being a child of God, a daughter of the almighty creator of the universe. I experience His love lavished upon me as I journey through life. His love makes me feel secure and special.

---

[70] Ephesians 1:4-5.
[71] Hebrews 13:20-21.
[72] Romans 10:9.
[73] I John 3:1.

Promises I Can Stand Upon

I stand upon what I believe. These promises from God knit together my personal theology. I have taken the Bible as a whole and honed it down to these four promises to define my creed of faith.

Imperishable Rebirth – The anchor of my faith that holds me safe and secure, sheltering me from the winds and storms of life, are based upon this promise: "You have been born anew, not of perishable seed but of imperishable, through the living and abiding word of God."[74] My salvation and regeneration by the Holy Spirit is not a passing fancy. My relationship with Christ is imperishable, which means it is enduring and indestructible. Nothing can take it away from me—it is permanent, and I stand securely upon this truth.

Living Free – This promise of God releases me from the entanglement of sin and relieves me of the heavy guilt of sin. The disciple John wrote, "If the Son has set you free, you will be free indeed."[75] When God forgives me of my sin, it is gone. We have been set free by Christ, and we owe it to Him to live as free people. It would break His heart if we lived as though we still needed to carry the weight of sin around like a boulder on our back.

Emmanuel – A pearl of Scripture that wraps me in God's presence like a warm blanket on a cold night is found in the words Jesus spoke before He left Earth to return to Heaven: "Lo, I am with you always, even to the end of the world."[76]

I have always been a chicken in the truest sense of the word. When I was young, I was easily frightened. I even slept with a baton under my bed! Until my husband died, I had never lived alone in my life. I still get startled at night when I hear odd noises (*especially those from my ice maker which sounds like clunky feet taking slow steps*). My imagination runs wild, and I get jumpy. Perhaps this is the reason I cherish the promise of Emmanuel: that God is always with us. I am

---

[74] I Peter 1:23.
[75] John 8:36.
[76] Matthew 28:20.

never alone. I do not have to be afraid. Some people count sheep, but I repeat this verse over and over, and it brings beautiful slumber.

All Things Good – This benediction is one of the major tenets of my faith: "We know that in everything God works for good with those who love Him, who are called according to His purpose."[77] John and I learned many hard lessons during his battle with leukemia, but we stood on this promise of God. It sustained us through our darkest hours. We fervently believed that if John did not survive his dreadful disease that God would still use it for good. I cannot tell you the countless ways our family has seen the fruit of this conviction. John's walk of faith during great suffering touched many lives. Countless individuals shared with our family how they reevaluated their faith and grew closer to the Lord after witnessing John's trust in God every step of the way. The profound heaviness of our loss is lightened as we see God's continued redeeming touch.

Promises I Depend Upon Daily

There is not a day that passes when I am not wholly dependent upon the promises of God. These specific gems help me maximize the gift of each day. These promises remove worry and doubt from my life and enable me to savor each moment.

Clean Heart – Every morning I am restored as God works His wonder in my life. "Create in me a clean heart, O God, and put a new and right spirit within me."[78] Whatever happened yesterday is over. Each day, God produces a clean heart and righteous spirit within me so that I am open to receive whatever He desires for me. This promise equips me to participate in the work of His kingdom, in ways big and small.

Direction – A Bible verse I memorized as a little girl reassures me of God's guidance and direction as He daily sustains me. "Trust in the Lord with all your heart, lean not on your own understanding; in all your ways acknowledge Him,

---

[77] Romans 8:28.
[78] Psalm 51:10.

and He will direct your paths."[79] I need God's guidance to weigh decisions and make choices. He knows what is best for me. If I follow Him, I am headed in the right direction.

Refuge and Strength – This promise shelters and safeguards me, "God is our refuge and strength, a very present help in trouble."[80] A wonderful book I read years ago, *The Road Less Traveled* by M. Scott Peck, featured the most memorable first sentence I have ever read—"Life is difficult."[81] Trouble comes in all shapes and sizes. Difficulties can overwhelm. God gives me strength to overcome it all because I know He is my refuge and my strength. His power will conquer when my courage fails.

Peace – The promise of peace baffles unbelievers yet remains a fundamental element of living a life of faith in Christ, "The peace of God, which passes all understanding, will keep your hearts and minds in Christ Jesus."[82] When tragedy strikes and the bottom falls out from under us, we can know the kind of peace that the world may not comprehend. This peace transcends heartbreak, tragedy, and devastation. With God in control, peace can permeate within us despite our dire circumstances.

Promises of Hope and Future

Christians are people of hope. It is one of our distinguishing characteristics. Martin Luther King Jr. said, "We must accept finite disappointment, but we must never lose infinite hope."[83] These promises give me hope and help me see the bright, shining stars in the darkest of nights. God promises that my future is preordained, and I anticipate the glories that await me.

Heart's Desires – The tenderness of God is confirmed elegantly through the

---

[79] Proverbs 3:5-6.
[80] Psalm 46:1.
[81] M. Scott Peck, *The Road Less Traveled*, New York: Simon & Schuster, 1978, p. 1.
[82] Philippians 4:7.
[83] Dr. Martin Luther King Jr., "A Proper Sense of Priorities," speech delivered in Washington, DC, February 6, 1968.

Psalms. This promise shows that what is important to us is important to God. "Take delight in the Lord, and He will give you the desires of your heart."[84] It gives me hope to know that my Heavenly Father loves me and longs to bring my most precious desires to fruition.

His Intercession – There are times in life when hope is hard to grasp. Spending many lonely nights in a hospital, watching and waiting with John, overwhelmed me. There were times I wanted to pray, yet no words came. God understood. The Apostle Paul said, "The Spirit helps us in our weakness; for we do not know how to pray as we ought, but the Spirit Himself intercedes for us with sighs too deep for words."[85] When I am depleted, and the only thing left are my tears, the Holy Spirit advocates to God the Father on my behalf. He utters the prayers that my own spirit cannot muster.

Being with God – Jesus painted a picture of our future life in Heaven when he shared:

"In my Father's house are many rooms; if it were not so, would I have told you that I go to prepare a place for you? And when I go and prepare a place for you, I will come again and will take you to myself, that where I am, you may be also."[86]

This promise plants the seed of expectation for Heaven in my heart. My brother-in-law Rob has reminded me many times of the truth in Ecclesiastes that, "God has set eternity in the human heart."[87]

I long to one day bask in the never-ending presence of God. I yearn to sit at the feet of Jesus. I have a long list of topics I want to discuss. I will have a richly filled eternity singing with the angels, giving praise and glory to God. The

---

[84] Psalm 37:4.
[85] Romans 8:26.
[86] John 14:2-3.
[87] Ecclesiastes 3:11.

anticipation of being with God for eternity is what drives and motivates me in this journey of faith.

Completion – God's Word assures me that my journey of faith will come to a final, full conclusion. "I am sure that He who began a good work in you will bring it to completion at the day of Jesus Christ."[88] I know assuredly that the moment my precious husband took his last breath, John was immediately healed. He was with God. He no longer endured the crushing disease that ravaged his body for two years. He was whole and healthy again. His life of devotion and faith was complete.

This promise undergirds my future. When I reach Heaven, all my highest intentions, best attempts, and near-miss moments will be over. In God's eyes, I will be fully finished and lacking in nothing.

What does God want you to know about Him? That He keeps His promises. What promises can you incorporate into your life that you can bank upon? Stand upon? Depend upon? Hope upon? Claim His promises and cling to them, for they are the lifeblood of our faith.

---

[88] Philippians 1:16.

Questions for Reflection

* What promises of God do you believe you can bank your life upon?

* What promises of God do you believe you can stand upon?

* What promises of God do you depend upon daily?

* What promises of God offer you hope and a future?

CHAPTER TEN

"I See Inside Your Heart"

I have always enjoyed playing the card game solitaire. I have never played the game on a computer; I prefer an old-fashioned deck of cards. Recently, I heard a guest speaker at a business conference make a startling statement about this one-person game—according to her, seven out of ten people admit to cheating at solitaire.

How ludicrous this seems. There is no other opponent! Why would anyone cheat against themselves? It is not like you won't know you are cheating. Is it possible that people can pretend so well that they actually start to believe the lie?

Young children love to pretend. When I was growing up, my brothers devised all kinds of games where we pretended to be somewhere far more exciting than our backyard. We would be fugitives on the lam, running from the police, trying to find a way back home before we were caught. We would be at war, and we had to sneak up on the enemy before they snuck up on us. We were pirates on a ship searching for land.

Likewise, when my own children were young, they loved to create games of pretending. One of their favorites they called "Hot Lava." My three rascals would pull every pillow and cushion off every chair and couch in our home and scatter them randomly on the floor. They pretended to be island hopping, jumping from cushion to cushion. Whenever one of them stumbled off and landed on the floor, they pretended to be drowning in scalding hot lava. Oh, the drama that ensued as that unfortunate child lost the game.

As a parent, it is important to teach children the difference between what is real and pretend. As they grow older and develop, their sense of reality becomes more acute. I wish I could say that once we become adults, we cease to pretend. Obviously if the statistic about cheating in solitaire is any indication, we haven't fully given up on pretending. And if we are pretending with ourselves, we are most likely pretending with others as well.

Psychologists tell us that some people "create their own reality." They pretend to be something or someone they are not, and eventually they start believing it. They can even convince those around them to believe their false pretense.

We might be able to pretend with ourselves, and even with others, but can we pretend with God? Many of us try, and probably more often than we care to admit. But one of the intrinsic attributes of God is omniscience. He is all-knowing about everything, everybody and everywhere, all over the world, all at the same time. It's a mind-boggling aspect of our Creator.

Maybe we think we can get away with pretending with God because the complexity of His knowledge is so vast. We play games with our own minds, thinking perhaps, God has so many people to watch, I am sure He won't notice me this one time. But our logic trips up in this very fact—God is often looking more closely at us on the inside, rather than on the outside. He discerns our thoughts and motives, which are far more revealing than our mere outward actions.

In the Old Testament, God instructed the priest Samuel to anoint the new king of Israel. He sent him to the home of Jesse, a respected man in the community who had eight sons. God instructed the priest Samuel to meet and inspect each of Jesse's sons to select and anoint one as Israel's future king. Initially, Samuel was drawn to the tall, muscular Eliab who had the regal look of a king. But God warned Samuel saying, "Do not look on his appearance, or on the height of his stature, because I have rejected him; for the Lord sees not as man sees; man looks on the outward appearance, but the Lord looks on the heart."[89]

After hearing God's voice speak to his inward being, Samuel scrutinized all eight of Jesse's sons. He finally realized that God's choice was David—the least likely of all—according to traditional kingly standards. He was short in stature and the youngest in the family, a rare choice for such a highly anointed position. Samuel did not find David inside his father's home waiting to be considered for this important position; rather, he found him outside in the dirty fields tending his father's flock of sheep.

God does not look at people and circumstances through the same lens as we do. Sometimes the most obvious answer to our problem is not the one God knows will be best for us. God looks inside our heart. He sees not just who we are now, but also who we can become. He knows our potential. He knows how different our lives will look once we trust Him and allow His strength and grace to permeate within us. Becoming the person God wants us to be requires being truehearted and living a life of transparency. Playing no games. No more pretending.

God knows all our thoughts—the shallow ones that creep up by the minute, as well as the more hidden ones we have pondered for years. He knows our inner workings and how our thoughts can escalate from mere fleeting whims to serious plotting. The psalmist proclaims, "O Lord, you have searched me and you know me...you perceive my thoughts from afar."[90]

An interesting relationship exists between our thoughts and actions. The connector between these two elements is motive. Our motives propel us to

---

[89] I Samuel 16:7.
[90] Psalm 139:1-2.

behave in a certain way. Even though we trick ourselves into believing that our motives are invisible, God sees them. He peers into them, perhaps even more than into our actions. He cares deeply about why we do what we do. Actions can look noble on the outside, yet they can be shallow on the inside. What compels us to do what we do? God looks inside our heart and clearly sees our motives. We may try to hide our motives from ourselves and others, but we can never hide them from Him.

If I decide to give much-needed money to a family who has been struggling with finances, that may seem like a kind action on my part. But what if I am really doing it so that I can tell my friends about it, so that they will think I am a caring, generous person? Is the act motivated more by my concern for my reputation than by the struggling family's genuine need? What if in the process I have ruined the family's dignity and self-esteem by sharing their private situation with others? Then, my seemingly good deed is rendered shallow in the eyes of God.

If my action does not spring from an authentic attitude of service, I may be fooling myself and those around me. God may discern that it was selfish pride that conceived the whole plan. He sees right through me.

We all pretend for different reasons. We play games with ourselves, and we try to play them with God. For example, let us look at worship. Sometimes we wake up on Sunday morning, and we don't feel "in the mood" to go to church. Perhaps we had a tough week and felt distant from God. Down deep inside, we know that our soul is usually best rejuvenated when we are surrounded by God's beautiful creation. But we decide to go to church anyway. Probably out of guilt. There, we mumble through the liturgy, half-sing the songs, and tune out the sermon. Our mind wanders during the prayers. We can't get to the car fast enough. It's an empty experience; yet we tell ourselves we earned favor with God because we went through the motions. Why do we pretend with God?

Perhaps our time could have been better spent. Maybe we could have hiked in a park, walked on a lonely beach, or watched a sunset over a lake. The choice to spend quiet time alone with God might have been a wiser, more genuine decision. Heartfelt worship is when we give God our full attention. An old adage captures this beautifully: "It is better to go fishing and think about God than to go to church and think about fishing."

Sometimes in the name of God, or in the name of the church, we do good things with impure motives. We teach, preach, and proclaim the gospel to the world. We work hard and appear outwardly to be doing everything right. Time has shown that despite Christians' good attempts, we commit outrageous mistakes. We have seen nationally renowned TV evangelists arrested for fraud, and pastors dispelled for conducting illicit affairs. In my hometown, our local newspaper chronicled an embezzlement of church funds by a congregation's financial administrator. These public scandals bite with a poisonous sting. We know the world is watching. Impure motives can create dark stains upon our attempts to be Christ's light in the world.

Many of us serve in the local church and charitable organizations, but our misguided motives do not make headlines. Our secret thoughts will most likely be overlooked by others, but God is aware of them. He knows what motivates us—is it self-interest? Pride? Power?

In Proverbs, we learn, "All the ways of a man are pure in his own eyes, but the Lord weighs the spirit."[91] We might trick ourselves into believing that our motives are pure, but God will look where no one else can see. He examines our spirit, deep in the place where our genuine motives simmer. We may think our motives will stay hidden forever, but the Bible says this:

"For the Word of God is living and active, sharper than any double-edged sword; it penetrates even to dividing soul and spirit, joints and marrow, it judges the thoughts and attitudes of the heart. Nothing in all creation is hidden from God's sight."[92]

---

[91] Proverbs 16:2.
[92] Hebrews 4:12-13.

The best way I know to eliminate impure motives is to be proactive in creating fresh, new motives. My friend Clint, who leads the Information and Technology Department at a large law firm, always tells me regarding data, "Garbage in, garbage out." I think this is true about life as well. If we fill our minds with negative, unproductive, and distasteful information, then all the space within us gets filled up with junk. How can anything positive, fulfilling, or God-glorifying possibly come from within us? Garbage in, garbage out.

The key lies in filling our minds with things of higher substance. The Apostle Paul wrote to the believers in Rome, encouraging them to do just this, "Be transformed by the renewal of your mind, that you may prove what is the will of God, what is good and acceptable and perfect."[93]

It is possible to renew our minds! We have a choice of what we allow to enter our thoughts. We can be our own gatekeeper, asking God to plant self-control deeply within us. We can turn off negative TV programs; we can refuse to see films that glorify violence; we can stop listening to people who tell jokes that belittle others. We can choose to stop buying publications that print lies and slander. In a positive, proactive approach, we can choose to create a new foundation in our mind. How? By saturating our thought-life with elements that strengthen our faith. God's Word encourages us to do the following:

> *"Make every effort to supplement your faith with virtue, and virtue with knowledge, and knowledge with self-control, and self-control with steadfastness, and steadfastness with godliness, and godliness with brotherly affection, and brotherly affection with love. For if these things are yours and abound, they keep you from being ineffective or unfruitful in the knowledge of our Lord Jesus Christ."*[94]

If we take this instruction to heart and retrain our thought patterns, then our motives will, over time, become pure. We can focus on these attributes to

---

[93] Romans 12:12.
[94] II Peter 1:5-8.

build our character, draw us closer to God, and enable us to live stronger lives of integrity.

Our positive thoughts will spring forth godly motives, which in turn, will bear the fruit of holy, righteous behavior. Our actions will become authentic and transparent. We will welcome God's examination as He gently discerns our hearts, for we are confident He will find genuine love and compassion fueling our motives and driving our actions.

What does God want you to know about Him? That He sees inside your heart. Think about this the next time you play Solitaire.

Questions for Reflection

* Have you ever tried to pretend with yourself or with God? What was the result?

* The author asserts in this chapter that "Our motives propel us to behave in a certain way." Do you agree with her? How have you seen this evidenced in your life, or in the life of others?

* Have you ever done something that on its own merit is deemed "a good thing," yet you did it with an impure motive? How did that make you feel?

* The author shares, "The best way I know to eliminate impure motives is to be proactive in creating fresh, new motives." What ways can you try to do this in your life?

CHAPTER ELEVEN

"I Can Work With Anyone"

If you were God, what kind of people would you choose to help carry out your sovereign will and holy plans to redeem humanity? I have given this a lot of thought. If I were God, I would make a list of required attributes for people to have before I chose them. My list would include the following:

Maturity
Responsibility
Dependability
High morals
Eloquence
Strong leadership
Confidence
Keen decisiveness

After studying the Bible for many years, I have realized that it is a good thing that I am not God! If He had implemented my criteria, we would have missed out on the colorful stories of Noah, Abraham, Ruth, David, Mary, Peter, Mary Magdalene, and Paul, these great pillars of our faith.

As we view Biblical history, we see a significant principle of how God operates: He always does the unexpected. When we study the stories of the people who God secured to bring about His plan for the world, we are humbled. We stand in awe at how God worked with each one, providing the strength, wisdom, and power needed, regardless of their tarnished pasts, physical ailments, emotional hang-ups, or tainted pedigrees. God is in the business of turning nobodies into somebodies.

"For consider your call, brothers, not many of you were wise according to worldly standards, not many were powerful, not many were of noble birth; but God chose what is foolish in the world to shame the wise, God chose what is weak in the world to shame the strong."[95]

Anyone can be instrumental to God—and He often chooses to use the least likely candidates according to the world's standards. Some of God's earliest leaders in the Old Testament had major flaws. They repeatedly made poor choices, but God worked with them despite their many weaknesses to further His will for the world.

Abraham frequently lied and sought control rather than trust God to deliver on His promises. But when he was one hundred years old, God blessed Abraham with a son, and he fathered the new nation of Israel, beginning the biological and spiritual legacy of God's chosen people.

Jacob devised a cunning plot against his dying father Isaac. He disguised himself as his brother Esau and tricked his father into granting the sacred blessing to him, rather than to his brother who was the first born and rightful heir. Nevertheless, God chose to continue his nation's line through Jacob, blessing him with twelve sons, who eventually became the Twelve Tribes of Israel.

---

[95] I Corinthians 1:26-27.

Moses had a speech impediment, was rather shy, and felt downright awkward in a leadership role. That did not seem to matter to God because He empowered Moses to confront and convince the powerful Pharoah of Egypt to release the Israelites from slavery. With boldness and courage he did not know he possessed, Moses led God's people out of Egypt to freedom. It was into Moses' hands that God entrusted His holy law on Mount Sinai.

King David broke most of the Ten Commandments, but despite his propensity for horrific sin, God shaped him to become the greatest king in Israel's history. God chose to honor David by blessing his bloodline with the birth of Jesus, the promised Messiah, forty-two generations after his death. Biblical history remembers David as "a man after God's own heart."[96]

King Solomon, David's heir to the throne, indulged himself with seven hundred wives and three hundred concubines (*John and I used to laugh that this is perhaps where the term "king-size bed" originated*). Despite his indiscretions, God blessed him with the great gift of wisdom. Solomon's practical advice and adages are recorded in the book of Proverbs, and they have inspired millions of people through the ages. Solomon gained the vision and tenacity to build the Lord a glorious temple on Mount Zion in Jerusalem. This spectacular place of worship stood for over 400 years.

God's hand continued to work with unlikely individuals at the dawn of history in the New Testament era.

John the Baptist was an eccentric character who wore wild clothing made of camel hair and a leather girdle around his waist. He lived in the desert wilderness and devoured locusts and wild honey for dinner. God used this radical man as the great forerunner of Jesus Christ, preaching the repentance of sin and baptism. John was blessed to announce the Messiah's arrival.

Simon was a rough, hardened fisherman. Despite his tempestuous personality and lack of education, God molded him into the leader of the disciples and

---

[96] I Samuel 13:14.

the first head of the early church. Jesus changed his name to Peter, which means "solid rock." His passion and zeal continued throughout his life, and he carried the gospel to the ends of the earth, dying a martyr's death for his devotion to God.

Saul of Tarsus was clearly an unlikely candidate to spread the gospel. As a devout Jew, he hated Christians with a passion and sought to destroy the name of Jesus. He obtained authority and official paperwork from the high priest to have believers bound and taken to Jerusalem for certain death. God saw within Saul a passion that could be rechanneled for good.

Following a radical encounter with the resurrected Christ, Saul was never the same again. God changed his name to Paul, and he became a dynamic missionary, taking the gospel to the Gentiles. He penned thirteen of the twenty-seven books in the New Testament, leaving a vast spiritual legacy.

And in modern history, God continues to work in the lives of many—often using those who, according to the world's standards, might not possess the most stellar credentials.

C.S. Lewis was a British novelist, poet, medievalist, and literary critic. As a devout agnostic, he was outspoken about the improbability of God's existence. His lectures often warned individuals of great intellect not to fall prey to the Bible's teachings. But when Lewis reached middle age, God began to stir within his mind and heart. A dear friend of Lewis, J.R.R. Tolkien, a Christian and fellow medieval writer, began to prick Lewis' intellectual curiosity about the authenticity and reliability of The Bible. Tolkien nurtured a budding faith in his friend, proclaiming the truth of God's Word. Once converted, Lewis authored some of the greatest theological writings in modern Christian literature, including Mere Christianity, The Screwtape Letters, and The Chronicles of Narnia.

Charles Colson was a member of President Nixon's inner circle and a key orchestrator of the Watergate scandal in the 1970s. He was sent to federal prison where he became a believer, much to the scorn of the Christian community, many of whom doubted his sincerity. But God knew Colson's heart was pure and that his conversion was authentic. Colson became an evangelic Christian leader and founded Prison Fellowship, a national organization that ministers to the families of inmates. He also penned an extensive list of insightful books to encourage believers in their faith.

Anne Lamott is a recovered alcoholic, single mother, and sufferer of clinical depression. She is extremely outspoken about politics and issues of social justice, often offending some Christians with her candor and crass use of language. Perhaps it is precisely because of these characteristics that God has enabled her to be profoundly effective in sharing the gospel. Lamott has written many books that chronicle her journey of faith. Her down-to-earth style appeals to everyday people who may never read a book by a more traditional Christian author.

Isaiah wrote, "For my thoughts are not your thoughts, neither are your ways my ways, says the Lord. For as the heavens are higher than the earth, so are my ways higher than your ways and my thoughts than your thoughts."[97] Never second guess God's ways. The Lord will select whomever He chooses to join Him in His plan. It is futile to question the mind of God. Never underestimate how He will employ individuals to perform His labors.

God calls ordinary people to make a difference in the world. It happens every day, yet some of us hold back, unwilling to take a chance. We fear that our experiences may serve as roadblocks to God. Think again.

God Does Not Judge Us For Our Past Condition

We have explored many examples of individuals in the Bible who had complex, treacherous pasts. The common thread we share with them is that we all need a Savior. Once we accept the gift God offers of redemption through Christ, He washes away our past. The Bible refers to this transformation as our "new birth." When we are made new by God, our past condition is inconsequential in His eyes.

---

[97] Isaiah 55:8-9.

God Knows Our Present Circumstances

We all bring specific assets and liabilities to the table. As imperfect people, we will never "have it all together" in terms of feeling ready for God to enlist us. But God fills us with the knowledge and strength needed to carry out His tasks. God meets us right where we are, amid our present circumstances. He equips us to accomplish great things for Him.

God Loves Us For Our Personal Characteristics

I believe it is time to get over comparing ourselves to others. It does not matter if someone is more eloquent, popular, or appealing. God does not care if our personality is type A or type B. He desires to utilize all the gifts within the body of believers to achieve His will. Comparing ourselves to others can make us feel inferior and lead us to doubt our own capabilities. God wants to recruit us exactly as we are so that His glory will be made manifest through us.

God Forgives Our Potential Inadequacies

God is not looking for spiritual powerhouses. He seeks out individuals who have faith and a willingness to follow Him. It is that simple—no need to complicate it because God certainly does not. Perhaps He may yearn to place us in a role—not despite our weaknesses, but rather because of them. Why? Because it is then that we learn to become wholly dependent upon Him for our strength. The Apostle Paul shares this morsel of truth revealed to him after a session of complaining to God about his shortcomings. "Then the Lord said, 'My grace is sufficient for you, for my power is made perfect in weakness.'"[98]

What does God want you to know about Him? That He can work with anyone. Give Him a chance to capture your willing spirit. He will surprise and delight you with His handiwork.

---

[98] II Corinthians 12:9.

Questions for Reflection

* Are you surprised that God often uses the "least likely candidates" to further His will? Why do you think He does this?

* The author shared eight different stories of people in the Bible who God used despite their weaknesses. Which story resonated most with you and why?

* How does it make you feel that God does not judge us for our past condition? How can this make a difference in being used by Him today?

* Have you ever considered that God wants to use you to build up His Kingdom on earth?

CHAPTER TWELVE

"I Love to Celebrate!"

Life is enriched when we mark milestones and special occasions with a deliberate pause. Commemorating and celebrating moments of gladness, victories, and blessings is healthy and fulfilling.

I am blessed to have married into the Brannan family, an abundant, boisterous, large clan filled with much laughter and joy. My parents-in-law knew the deep sense of delight in raising a godly, happy brood. My husband was one of six children, and our children are three of nineteen grandchildren. As of this writing, we have twelve great-grandchildren in the family.

In the Brannan family, there are frequent celebrations—birthdays, births of new babies, baptisms, confirmations, music recitals, graduations, anniversaries, sports awards, performances, weddings, holidays, promotions, ordinations, and swearing-in ceremonies. For twenty-eight years, we celebrated our vacation time together on a large lake in North Carolina for a week each summer. Our family has been knit together in love for four generations, marking life's significant moments. This created bountiful traditions and loving bonds.

We learn in The Bible that God is purposeful about His celebrations. From the very beginning, God paused to acknowledge success and accomplishment throughout the process of creation.

> *"And God said, 'Let there be light', and there was light. And God saw that the light was good...God called the dry land Earth and the waters that were gathered together He called seas. And God saw that it was good...God saw everything that He had made, and behold it was very good."*[99]

God set a fine example for us in the way He chose to pause throughout Creation to recognize and commemorate the completion of stages and the goodness of His work.

It brings God glory when we stop to thank Him for His hand in our accomplishments, to give Him our praise and gratitude. To recognize that we are nothing without God is the secret to living a humble life, one that brings honor to God. As the disciple Peter taught in his first epistle, "Clothe yourselves, all of you, with humility toward one another, for God opposes the proud, but gives grace to the humble."[100] Acknowledging the involvement of God in your success builds strong memories of His role in your accomplishments and plants contentment in your heart.

The Old Testament tells how God designed feasts and festivals to observe important spiritual milestones and share merriment among the people. Beginning in the spring, there were seven Jewish feasts: Passover, the Feast of Unleavened Bread, the Feast of First Fruits, the Feast of Weeks, the Feast of Trumpets, the Day of Atonement, and the Feast of Tabernacles. In addition to the feasts, there were festivals and holy days to mark pivotal points in Israel's history, including Purim, Rosh Hashanah, Yom Kippur, Sukkot, and Hanukkah. God loves to celebrate, and He created His people to enjoy the act of celebration.

---

[99] Genesis 1:3; v10; v31.
[100] I Peter 5:5.

Jesus told a series of stories around a central theme of being lost. In the first parable, he told about a shepherd charged with tending one hundred sheep. After keeping count (*can you imagine having that job?*), the shepherd realized one of the sheep was missing. He left the ninety-nine to go search for the one lost sheep. When he found the sheep, the shepherd carried it on his shoulders, reveling in delight the entire way back to the flock. Once home, he decided to throw a party, inviting his friends and neighbors, saying, "Rejoice with me for I have found my sheep which was lost." Jesus concludes his story, saying, "Just so, I tell you, there will be more joy in Heaven over one sinner who repents than over ninety-nine righteous persons who need no repentance."[101]

Jesus then tells of a woman who had ten silver coins. Sadly, she misplaced one. She lit the lamp and began to sweep furiously all over her house to find the lost coin. Her diligence paid off, and she finally found her prized possession. Just like the shepherd, the woman decides that it is time to throw a party. She gathers her friends and neighbors to celebrate finding her coin. Jesus again reminds us, "Just so, I tell you, there is joy before the angels of God over one sinner who repents."[102]

What a wonderful way to illustrate what causes God and the angels to celebrate in Heaven. When a child of God repents of their sin and turns toward Him, a celestial party begins! These are cheerful, joyous occasions for the Lord. The Bible tells us, "God desires all men to be saved and to come to the knowledge of the truth."[103] Fortunately, men, women, boys, and girls are coming to the Lord every day—that tells me that God is in a perpetual state of partying and rejoicing.

Today, many churches observe Communion, also called The Lord's Supper or The Eucharist, to symbolize the Passover meal Jesus shared with his disciples

---

[101] Luke 15:3-7.
[102] Luke 15:8.
[103] I Timothy 2:4.

the night of his betrayal and arrest. Eating the bread and drinking the wine reminds us that Jesus gave us the ultimate gift: his body and blood to shed for the forgiveness of our sins.[104] Even though Communion is a somber event, we are filled with gratitude for the gift of salvation. As we partake, it is important to pause to thank God for this miracle of eternal life. Communion should be a moment of celebration in the life of every believer.

As parents, we tried to incorporate as many celebrations as possible for our children. When I look back upon the years of their childhood, some of my favorite memories were celebrating simple milestones in their lives. When John Jr. won a spelling bee at school, I baked a cake to celebrate his victory. When Mark became the first snaggletooth in the family, we celebrated with a spontaneous trip to the ice cream parlor. A few months later, we filmed him singing "All I Want for Christmas is My Two Front Teeth," and that video clip is one of our most treasured favorites. When Laura had surgery at age four, we celebrated her homecoming from the hospital with balloons, music, and dancing. She forgot all about the bandages on her little head.

I believe God wants us to celebrate the spiritual milestones in our lives as well. Have you ever struggled over trying to break a nasty habit? I know I have. One year during Lent, I decided to give up negative thoughts. Each time I had a negative thought, I wrote it down on a piece of paper. I then said a prayer and asked God to take away the thought from my mind. I tore the paper into tiny pieces and threw it away. On Easter morning, I celebrated that with God's help I was able to conquer negative thinking. After forty days of Lent, it became a habit to think positively instead of defaulting to the negative. I rejoiced! You should have seen all the chocolate eggs I ate that Easter morning to celebrate!

Our church makes a big deal about welcoming new members into our fold. We want them to feel loved and accepted, and we want to help them acclimate and become involved in the church family. Throughout their membership ses-

---

[104] Luke 22:19-20.

sions, we host a series of dinner parties at members' homes so they can get to know fellow church members. We mix it up generationally so that we all break out of the normal tendencies to interact with people from within our own age group. On the Sunday that new members are presented before the congregation, we give them a standing ovation. We hold a reception with frothy church punch and home-baked sweets. We take their pictures and decorate the bulletin boards around the church hallways with their smiles. We publish their personal stories of faith in the church newsletter. The celebration marks our gratitude that God is growing our church and enables the new members to feel our love. I know this brings delight to God.

Jesus once compared the Kingdom of Heaven with a wedding banquet. The joining of two people together to become a family is cause for great celebration. This past fall my daughter Laura married Joe, the love of her life, under a big tent in the middle of a huge pasture in South Carolina at the farm of her beloved godparents. Joe's mother Megan and I reflected afterward that the entire evening felt magical. I said it felt like "a tentful of love." Weddings celebrate love. Heaven will celebrate love.

What does God want you to know about Him? That He loves to celebrate. It gives God immense joy when one of His children comes home. It pleases Him when we celebrate His goodness in our lives.

Questions for Reflection

* Have you traditionally thought about God as being one who loves to celebrate? How did this chapter influence your images of God?

* Have you ever considered finding a way to celebrate spiritual milestones in your life? What are some ways you would enjoying exploring this?

* Do you regard Holy Communion as a celebration? Do you believe the church could gain by emphasizing this element of the sacrament? How?

* What are ways you can begin to celebrate God's goodness in your life?

CHAPTER THIRTEEN

"I Am Enough"

In consumer-driven cultures like America, people never seem satisfied. Just when you think you have purchased the most current, up-to-date cell phone or device, you turn around a week later, and your product suddenly feels archaic when you see its new and improved model. How were you supposed to know? The purchase that a mere week ago put a spring in your step as you walked out of the store now looks passé. It appears dowdy and downright old. We are never satisfied. No matter what we own, it never seems to be enough.

What does it mean to have enough? In considering this concept, let us reflect upon both quantity and scope. We need to evaluate our demands, needs, and expectations. How do you define "enough" in your own life? Is anything ever enough to completely satisfy you and not leave you hoping for more?

I write these words during the Covid-19 pandemic. At the onset of the virus, people started to panic. They stocked up on essential household items like toilet paper, laundry detergent, and canned goods. Supplies could not meet the demand. Thus erupted the "toilet paper crisis" (I *don't believe I have ever strung those three words together before.*) I was baffled. Did everyone really need this much toilet paper? How did people form these outrageous expectations and demands leading them to horde? It struck me that if everyone simply purchased only the amount they truly needed, there would be no scarcity.

Another word for "enough" might be "sufficient." This is a hard concept for me to resolve when I relate this idea to food preparation. If I am cooking a chicken dinner for eight people, I am not comfortable unless I have twelve pieces of chicken. My reasoning is that perhaps half of the guests will want a second piece, and if they do, I will be prepared. At the grocery store, I stand in the poultry aisle and contemplate if I have calculated correctly. I second-guess myself and wonder if my estimate is too conservative. I then buy sixteen pieces of chicken, in case everyone at the dinner party wants a second piece. This used to drive my mother-in-law crazy. Being a child of the Depression, she would have most likely bought six pieces of chicken for eight people and cut two in half—in case two guests might not want a whole piece. When is there a sufficient amount of food? When is "enough" truly enough?

The concept of sufficiency—the idea of having enough—takes on much more meaning when applied to our spiritual lives. Is God enough? Is His son Jesus Christ enough? Can God be present in my life with such quantity or scope, as to fully meet my demands, needs, and expectations? I think it is time for a spiritual evaluation.

I have never questioned the omnipotence of God. If I believe that He is the Creator of the world, then it seems to me that everything following creation must be so much easier for Him. I do not arrogantly come before God with a list of demands. I know He is aware of my genuine needs. His knowledge satisfies me because He is all-knowing; yet I grapple daily with my limited knowledge. He sees the past, present, and future, and I sometimes have a hard time looking further than five minutes from now. God has always provided what I need, even though His provision is often something different than what I desired or expected.

In this vein, the benediction found in Ephesians speaks to my heart:

"Now to Him who by the power at work within us is able to do far more abundantly than all that we ask or think, to Him be glory in the church, and in Christ Jesus to all generations, for ever and ever."[105]

I cling to this truth because anything God ever does for me is far better than I could ever ask or come up with on my own. He continues to surprise me, day by day, year by year with His abundance.

The events and experiences in our lives may vary in significance, with some being intensely profound while others are less important. Rarely do our lives contain excellence in all aspects at once. The challenge lies in striking a balance. Our goal is to achieve a degree of fulfillment in all areas, so that over many years of growth and maturation, we can view our life as a whole and deem it sufficient.

Going deeper with my spiritual inventory, my life is comprised of the many roles I play—mother, sister, daughter-in-law, aunt, cousin, sister-in-law, friend, neighbor, and volunteer. I take each role seriously, and I try to give the best I can to successfully fulfill each role. But it is difficult to achieve my best every single day, in each capacity. Sometimes I go to bed at night, lamenting, I was a good mother today but a terrible sister. I tried to be a good daughter-in-law, but I wasn't a very good neighbor. Satisfaction can be elusive. Can I ever be enough? Am I ever sufficient in anything?

Each of us longs in our heart and soul for significance. We want to believe that if we died tomorrow, our life would have mattered. We want to be confident that we indeed made a difference as we took up this small piece of real estate on Earth. When we look to our own accomplishments and successes, we will always fall short. Late at night, when we cannot sleep, beset by a feeling of emptiness, all our moments of accomplishment cannot fill the void.

---

[105] Ephesians 3:20.

When the doctors told John that there was no further hope of beating his cancer, he began to reflect on what an extraordinary life God had given him. As a man who worked diligently in his career as an accountant and served our community with zeal, he realized that the highlights of his life were found more in simple things.

He reminisced about the hundreds of times we walked on the beach and enjoyed a lovely sunset. He laughed when he recalled getting lost on several trips in Europe but loved how we always ended up in a better place than we originally intended to go. He recalled moments of coaching our sons John Jr. and Mark in baseball, soccer, and football and the fun of teaching our daughter Laura to ride a bike. He shared that some of his most treasured times were "just showing up" at our kids' many activities and the joy of watching each of them grow up.

Some of John's sweetest memories were sitting around our dinner table as a family, laughing together and telling stories. Late one night upon reflection, he said, "Kim, how could I possibly ask God for more? I've been given so much—more than enough. I have had a lifetime of goodness and blessing. God has shown abundance to me my entire life. How could we have survived the past two years without His grace? He has been with us every step of the way. I simply cannot ask God for more."

People talk about the importance of checking off a "bucket list" before they die, but I can assure you that the extravagant, lofty items never rank at the top of life's greatest memories. It is the simple moments of basking in God's blessings of family and good friends. When our life comes to an end, true sufficiency might surprise us.

The opposite of enough is emptiness. When we feel empty, we don't have enough inside to satisfy us. When we are physically hungry, our stomach growls because it needs food to fill up the empty space. Spiritual hunger is when our soul craves peace. We need something outside of ourselves to complete us. We need—and long—to know satisfaction deep inside. We yearn for significance and fulness. Living with an empty soul feels like being on a journey that never gets us closer to our destination. The shallow place of unfulfillment weighs us down.

During his travels in Samaria, Jesus encountered a troubled woman as he sat by a well in the middle of the small village of Sychar. Due to centuries of political unrest between Jews and Samaritans, the woman was startled when Jesus spoke to her, asking for a drink as she drew water from the town's well.

"How is it that you, a Jew, asks a drink of me, a woman of Samaria? For Jews have no dealings with Samaritans."

Jesus answered her, "If you knew the gift of God, and who it is that is saying to you, 'Give me a drink,' you would have asked him, and he would have given you living water."

Her curiosity piqued, the woman replied, "Sir, you have nothing to draw with, and the well is deep; where do you get that living water?"

The woman would remember for the rest of her life the words Jesus spoke next. She would never be the same again. "Everyone who drinks of this water will thirst again; but whoever drinks of the water that I shall give will become a spring of water welling up to eternal life."

The woman said, "Sir, give me this water that I may not thirst." Then Jesus began to speak with her, revealing how much he knew about her life—the good, the bad, and the ugly. He told her, "I know you have had five husbands and the man who you are living with now is not your husband." This was a scandalous breaking of the law in her day. She was amazed at His knowledge since they were strangers; yet He knew her history. The woman was even more astonished that He did not judge her, nor look down upon her.[106]

Jesus' living water was offered with the promise to completely fill the deep places within her heart and soul, where she had always felt a hollow emptiness. No man, no relationship had ever quenched her thirst for genuine love, unmerited mercy, and an outpouring of grace. This was the kind of love that would truly last—no betrayal, no desertion, which was all she had ever known. After

---

[106] John 4:7-29.

five husbands, she was still seeking genuine, unconditional love and satisfaction.

I believe the woman in this story represents all of us. We have "baggage" and "stuff" that we engage in, attempting to fill up the emptiness we feel. To find long-lasting fulfillment and peace, we search everywhere except for the one place that really matters. Only God is enough. Only God can fill us up so completely, so thoroughly with His grace, forgiveness, and love that our heart and soul will never hunger or thirst again. We don't have to earn His living water—it is freely and abundantly given.

Psalm 42 drives this message into my heart, "As a deer pants for flowing streams, so my soul longs for thee, O God. My soul thirsts for God, for the living God."[107] I simply cannot get enough of God's presence. We are only made complete in a relationship with Christ. To have Him is to have everything that has ever mattered. It is the only thing that can truly fill us up and offer lasting satisfaction.

As a child, one of my favorite Bible stories was of Jesus feeding the five thousand. I think I particularly enjoyed how it was a child, not a grown-up, who provided the five small loaves of bread and two fish that Jesus blessed and used to perform the miracle to feed the enormous crowd.[108] As an adult, I recognize new lessons in this simple story. The people had been outside all day listening to Jesus preach, so they were hungry as the hour grew late. In God's abundance, Jesus produced such a bounty of food that when everyone had feasted on all they could eat, the disciples collected twelve baskets of leftovers. What a morsel of wisdom this teaches—God desires to give us more than we can ever imagine. We long for sufficiency; yet He gives us abundance.

We are told that following the miracle, many were astonished, and some wondered about this man Jesus. Could he really have been sent from God? The Bible tells us that the people returned to their towns and villages, sharing the

---

[107] Psalm 42:1-2.
[108] John 6:5-14.

good news with others about a man who fed so many with so little.

What strikes me as odd in this story is what Jesus does after the miracle. He gets into a boat by Himself to cross the sea and withdraw to the mountains. One would think that he might linger, relish the moment, and chat with his disciples. If I had been Jesus, I would have wanted to receive accolades and "high fives" following the miracle I had just performed. Yet, Jesus does not. He seeks solitude.

We get a glimpse into Christ's thoughts by what happens the next day. Some people from the crowd eagerly returned to the exact same spot where Jesus had fed the multitude the day before. (*Those must have been some tasty fish sandwiches!*) Were they hoping He could repeat the miracle? When Jesus was not there, they boarded a boat to sail toward the other side of the sea where he had gone to spend time in the mountains. When they found Him, they asked, "Rabbi, when did you get here?" He answered:

"You are looking for me, not because you saw miraculous signs but because you ate the loaves and had your fill. Do not work for food that spoils, but for food that endures to eternal life, which the Son of Man will give you."[109]

Jesus wanted to do far more than feed bodies that would all soon perish. He came to nourish souls that could live forever. But the people only wanted more bread, more dazzling miracles.

It is so easy to stuff ourselves full by eating the world's cheap bread—success, achievements, money, comfort, and pleasure—things we consume because they take the edge off our spiritual hunger. So many of us are like sponges, soaking up the world's pleasures, with no space left for God.

Through the years, I have read articles about some of the world's wealthiest individuals. Each expressed in their own way the idea that money cannot buy

---

[109] John 6:25-27.

happiness. This elite group, with more personal wealth than they knew what to do with, understood that neither money nor success, nor anything the world can provide, will ever fill the emptiness in our souls.

Sometimes our enthusiasm for God begins to wane after many years. This is often a result of our decision to concentrate more time and energy toward less worthy pursuits. This should serve as a red flag to us, indicating that our spiritual appetite needs to be recalibrated. We can ask God to create a renewed sense of spiritual hunger in our lives. He can plant within us a new thirst for His presence. As long-time believers, it is wise to look back upon the zeal we had when we first became Christians. Our enthusiasm was contagious, and we simply could not get enough of God. We were delighted to grow and learn more in our faith each day.

Conducting a spiritual inventory is a healthy undertaking. Periodically, we need to ask ourselves, where is my joy? Am I still living the abundant life? If not, what can I do to recapture my passion? One of my favorite Bible verses addresses these questions: "Create in me a clean heart, O God, and put a new and right spirit within me. Restore to me the joy of Thy salvation. Uphold me with a willing spirit."[110]

As God creates in us a clean heart, one that is fresh and eager to draw closer to Him, He will also restore to us the original joy of our salvation found in Christ. He has done this repeatedly in my life. I am grateful each time because I immediately feel a renewed sense of hunger and thirst for Him.

We need to learn how to feed ourselves on Jesus—upon His life, His sacrifice, His word, His promises, and His power to work in our lives. Christ said, "I am the bread of life; he who comes to me shall not hunger, and he who believes in me shall never thirst."[111] We need to become spiritually hungry. We need to long for the way only God can fill us up.

What does God want you to know about Him? That He is enough. All

---

[110] Psalm 51:10, v12.
[111] John 6:35.

purpose, meaning, and value in life come from God. He alone is enough to fill our souls in abundance.

Questions for Reflection

* When have you recently caught yourself feeling unsatisfied? How did it feel?

* Have you ever thought about sufficiency as an element in your spiritual life? What role does it play?

* After sharing the Biblical account about the encounter Jesus had with the Samaritan woman, he met at the well, the author stated, "I believe the woman in this story represents all of us." In what ways? Can you personally relate to her?

* Following the story about Jesus feeding the five thousand, the author makes the statement, "We long for sufficiency; yet He gives us abundance." Share an example of when you have experienced this in your life.

CHAPTER FOURTEEN

"I Make All Things New"

T he most natural way I have found to introduce a young child to the Lord is by explaining in simple terms, "God made the world. God made you." It is a refreshing exercise of faith to remember these two basic facts. We know who God is by seeing what He made.

I have always loved to travel. I enjoy seeing how incredibly different cities, states, countries, and continents are from one another. I am amazed by God's sense of beauty. I never cease to be enthralled by His attention to detail in creation. He designed tall, rugged mountains carpeted with trees that seem to reach to the heavens. The oceans he shaped seem to be endless as far as the eye can see. God's sense of order is evidenced in the cycle of the tides and how they relate to the moon and its phases.

What a sense of organization He employed to bring together the universe in the way He aligned the planets in the Milky Way and set in motion the principles of physics like gravity, which keeps our feet firmly planted on the ground. His sunrises and sunsets are magnificent, utilizing a palette of blues, oranges, reds, purples, and yellows. Then, with artistic flair, God imbues an element of spontaneity in that no two are alike. God's creativity reflects His identity.

Once a creator, always a creator. God is in the business of creating. He began the world with a spoken word, and He never stopped creating once the world was made. He continued His craft in the lives of people.

The nation of Israel started with a promise God made to Abraham: to bless him with descendants and land. In his old age, Abraham was blessed with Isaac, his only son. Isaac fathered two sons, Esau and Jacob. Through God's creative work, it was Jacob who expanded the community of Israel through the birth of his twelve sons. These sons started their own families, and the branches of this nation grew and became known as the Twelve Tribes of Israel. These tribes became a mighty force in the world at that time.

When we look back upon history, Israel had its ups and downs in her relationship with God. When the people were obedient to God's commands, they experienced unity with one another. When they fell back into their sinful habits, they fell away from the love and harmony of earlier times. Centuries later, after the death of King Solomon, the tribes divided into two separate kingdoms. The first kingdom, consisting of the ten northern tribes with Samaria as its capital, kept the name "Israel." The second kingdom took the name "Judah," and it consisted of the two remaining tribes, Judah and Benjamin, which lay in the south, with Jerusalem as its capital.

In 586 B.C., the Babylonians, led by King Nebuchadnezzar, destroyed Jerusalem and the magnificent temple built by King Solomon. They carted the citizens of Judah into exile in Babylon. It was a bleak time in the history of God's people. Many chapters in the Old Testament communicate the laments of God's people. They voiced their frustration and confusion over their plight as exiles. Their land was in shambles, they had no roots, nor a temple for worship. They had forgotten that their God was a creator, that He still possessed His power to make things new. During these difficult, discouraging years, God used the prophet Isaiah to speak to the people on His behalf. Isaiah gave the people a reason to hope:

> "*Remember not the former things, nor consider the things of old, Behold, I am doing a new thing; now it springs forth, do you not perceive it? I will make a way in the wilderness and rivers in the desert. The ransomed of the Lord shall return, and come to Zion with singing; Everlasting joy shall be upon their heads; they shall obtain joy and gladness.*"[112]

Clearly, God was not yet done with His people. He was still reaching down into their pain and despair, hearing their cries. He took their present circumstances and formed new plans for their future.

God promised that a portion of the people, a remnant torn from the cloth of the nation, would return to Jerusalem and rebuild their country. He painted a picture for them to help visualize their future: a lush river stream gushing through the dry, arid desert where they lived. What a creative way to re-energize the broken spirit of His people, infuse new hope and enthusiasm into their lives, and give them a reason to wake up each day.

Not only did God continue in his role as creator throughout the history of the Israelites, but He continues to create in our lives today. This aspect of God's character is one of the attributes I love most about Him. Life is filled with trials and difficulties. The Bible never promises that trusting in God will prevent experiencing life's harsh realities. In fact, God's Word tries to prepare us for the inevitability that life will indeed be challenging. But putting our trust in the Lord will improve our odds of finding positive ways to deal with trouble and heartache.

When my brother Chuck was fifty years old, he suffered a massive brain-stem stroke. It was a devastating blow to him, his wife and children, and our entire extended family. Chuck was a gifted musician, playing the guitar and

---

[112] Isaiah 43:18-19.

singing, and was a natural handyman. He could build or repair anything. When he was a teenager, Chuck built a big, wooden deck in the back of our childhood home. No one taught Chuck how to build; he just figured it out. When our children were young, they called him "Uncle Fix Fix Fix" because every time he came to visit, Chuck would see something that looked awkward or defective to him, and he would just begin to repair it for me. He never waited to be asked.

The stroke Chuck experienced paralyzed him completely from the neck down. Never again would his hands use a screwdriver to tighten a loose bolt. Never again would he lead worship and praise music at his church. No more strumming his guitar or singing. He could not speak; he could not move; yet his mind was unaltered. I could tell by his big blue eyes that Chuck understood everything happening around him, but he could not participate in our conversations with the doctors and therapists. In the early phase, Chuck mustered all his strength to communicate through blinking his eyes. He blinked once for "yes" and twice for "no" to express his opinion on matters or to answer questions. But even this simple effort exhausted him.

It broke my heart to see my brother reduced to the life of a quadriplegic, utterly helpless, needing assistance for every basic need. His stay in the hospital lasted eight months. I sat with him throughout long days and lonely nights. There were times we thought he might not live through the night. But somehow, Chuck held on. God had a plan that none of us understood or could possibly imagine.

For many weeks Chuck was heavily sedated, and he was on a respirator to help him breathe. I sat by his bedside and read my Bible, searching for comfort and answers from God, while he slept peacefully next to me. Sometimes I read certain passages aloud in case he could hear them, hoping they would sink into his mind and heart.

One of my favorite Bible verses during those challenging days was a simple verse in one of my favorite psalms, "The Lord is near to the brokenhearted, and He saves the crushed in spirit."[113] The collective heart of our family was completely broken. We were painfully crushed in spirit. Chuck's prognosis was grave. The doctors told us that he would remain paralyzed for the rest of his life. He would be fed by a stomach tube because he had no working muscles to help him swallow. He would never speak again because he had no strength in his lungs to push the air up with enough effort to produce sound.

Our family decided that we had to adjust to "the new normal." Over time, the hospital stopped sending therapists to Chuck's home because they said he had reached a plateau. Thus, my amazing sister-in-law Wendy, Chuck's faithful wife, who keenly observed his therapy sessions, began conducting the therapies herself. When any of us went to visit, we massaged his legs, arms, and hands to relieve the muscles from drawing up and tightening. I learned how to feed him through his stomach tube. We went through the motions of caring for my brother with grateful hearts, happy that we still had him with us. His deep blue eyes flickered with his appreciation and the desire to live. We prayed hard and placed everything in God's hands. We asked for strength to go on. We asked for courage to hope for a brighter future for Chuck. I longed for God to make all things new for my brother, but I secretly wanted Chuck to return to the person he was before the stroke. That was not to be.

However, God's thoughts are always higher than our own, and His plans are always higher than our plans. God reached down into our heartache and frustration, into Chuck's weakened body, and slowly began His transformation. Progress began to crawl like a snail bringing its head out of the sand. We rejoiced over the small victories and gave God all our thanks and praise. Eventually, Chuck gained a tiny bit of movement in his right hand. It was just enough to enable him to operate a joystick on his electric wheelchair. This meant that he could have control over something in his life—Chuck could finally decide which room he wanted to be in and when he wanted to be in it. It was a huge

---

[113] Psalm 34:18.

breakthrough. Chuck's spirits and demeanor improved. He began to work on his facial muscles so that he could produce his winsome smile, with his deep dimples shining through. Chuck smiled often because he was incredibly grateful to God for his progress.

Several years passed. Chuck mastered the ability to swallow, thanks to continued treatment by Wendy, which opened the door to soft foods. After having nothing but liquid nutrition through a stomach tube for two years, Chuck beamed with delight when he tasted mashed sweet potatoes with brown sugar and butter. Chuck grinned from ear to ear as he slurped down chocolate pudding. Oh, the joy of tasting "real" food again! He was like a little boy on Christmas morning who finally received the bike he had wished for all year long.

God was slowly but surely making many things new for Chuck. He created a "new normal" that was not at all what my brother knew before but one that was so much greater than he hoped for during those long, dark months in the hospital. With God's help, Chuck defied all the odds of the doctor's dire predictions.

More years passed. Wendy kept diligently working with Chuck on basic language skills. After much trial and error, she taught him that if he reclined his wheelchair back as far as it would go, he could more readily push the air up from his lungs to form sounds. At first, his vocalizations were very guttural and hard to understand. However, just hearing him breathe loudly and grunt was music to our ears. God was working. The sounds grew more recognizable each day. Wendy would call me and hold the phone for Chuck to speak to me. I could understand some of it, and I loved hearing his voice. God was still busy creating in his life.

Two years later, we gathered at my brother's home for the Harvey family's Thanksgiving celebration. Before the meal was served, we circled around Chuck's wheelchair to hold hands, as we traditionally do before we pray. My husband John was about to ask grace, when Chuck looked at him and winked. With heads bowed, he reclined his wheelchair, and it was Chuck who offered up our Thanksgiving blessing to the Lord. His words were slow, pushing each word out with effort. I knew God was smiling. Tears of joy flowed down our faces. Chuck's words were evidence of God's handiwork.

It has now been fifteen years since Chuck's stroke. It has been a long journey, but we continue to see God's hand in his life. Last Christmas, Chuck's son Dane fashioned a device of sorts made from PVC pipe with a simple strap that holds Chuck's fingers wrapped over it. With Dane's invention, Chuck can navigate a computer keyboard by himself. The pipe gently "rolls" by the slight movement of his hand and allows his pointer finger to touch the proper keys. He now emails family and friends, surfs the internet to explore topics that intrigue him, connects with people on social media, and engages in online games with his old friends Pam, Karen, and Steve. To the dismay of Karen, Chuck usually beats her in Words with Friends. Last year, Chuck downloaded design software which he utilizes to create architectural drawings of health clubs and commercial buildings. God is not through with Chuck as He continues to take hopeless situations and turn them around. God plants within Chuck meaning and purpose for each day. My oldest brother would be the first to tell you that his life is full, and his soul is content.

Hope is one of the hallmarks of people of faith. For those who wander aimlessly in the world, never having made a connection with God, this concept must seem illusive. No matter how disappointing life may become, believers can cling to the hope we have in God the Father and in Jesus Christ our Lord. Some days we may feel as though all we can hold on to is a tiny shred of hope, but that is enough. God builds upon our hope and transforms individuals and circumstances.

The Apostle Paul experienced some of life's most dangerous and frightening situations as he carried the gospel to the ends of the known world. During his ministry he was shipwrecked, arrested, flogged, thrown in jail, and banished from towns he visited. Yet, in the middle of his turmoil, he continued to write to fellow believers encouraging them, "Rejoice in your hope, be patient in tribulation. Be constant in prayer."[114]

What does God want you to know about Him? That He makes all things new. He takes heartache and turns it into joy. He takes bitterness and converts it to trust. He takes fear and builds faith.

---

[114] Romans 12:12.

Questions for Reflection

* Have you ever thought about God continuing to create, following His creation of the world? What difference does this make in your understanding of God?

* Have you ever experienced a crisis in your life and wondered if God could possibly have a plan amid your difficulties? How did that make you feel?

* How did the story about the author's brother Chuck impact you? What did you learn from it about God's ability to make all things new?

* What would it take for you to trust God at His word, to begin to make all things new in your life?

CHAPTER FIFTEEN

"My Peace is Priceless"

The average number of hours in a work week in America continues to rise. Despite working more hours, even with the efficiencies that technology enables, people admit to feeling less fulfilled and more restless than ever before. The doors of mental health therapists and psychologists are swinging open to meet the need of all the people seeking help. They are searching for relief as they grapple with their deep sense of anxiety, worry, and unease.

It is difficult to put a price tag on the immeasurable gift of peace. I am referring to personal peace, the kind that dwells within our thoughts and emotions. We cannot know a deep sense of peace if we worry about issues over which we have no control or make comparisons that make us feel shallow.

The Bible shares many lessons about peace. God's Word provides sound teaching on how to seek and find this valuable treasure in our lives. The first step to laying a foundation for peace is to have a personal relationship with Christ. As Paul writes in the book of Romans, "Therefore, since we are justified by faith, we have peace with God through our Lord Jesus Christ."[115] Nothing can

---

[115] Romans 5:1.

compare to the knowledge and confidence we gain from the assurance of eternal salvation with God. This initiates the process for a lifelong pursuit of spiritual peace.

The prophet Isaiah long ago penned, "You will keep in perfect peace him whose mind is steadfast, because he trusts in you. Trust in the Lord forever, for the Lord is the rock eternal."[116] In this passage, the prophet describes the practice that leads to perfect peace—keeping our mind steadfast upon God. Another Biblical translation explains it as, "the one whose mind is stayed upon God."[117] A third version translates this passage as "the one whose thoughts turn often to the Lord."[118] To keep your mind stayed upon something requires concentration and discipline. It requires turning one's thoughts frequently to the Lord.

Many years ago, I took birthing classes when I was expecting our first child. One of the things I liked best about the Lamaze Method was its emphasis on how to manage the pain of contractions by hyper-focusing on a single object. I was taught to find something I wanted to look at in the room and stare at it intently, concentrating all my thoughts and energy upon that one object. I was able to do this during my actual labor, and it helped me overcome and manage the pain very effectively. I believe there are many parallels to this in our mind's attempt to focus fervently upon the Lord.

The reason Isaiah believed that keeping one's mind stayed upon the Lord led to peace was because he knew God was worthy of our trust. He referred to God as "an everlasting rock." Think of the immense massifs in places like the Grand Canyon or the Red Rocks of Arizona. God is even stronger and more unchanging than those colossal rocks. The prophet paints this image to explain why we can trust God—His strength and force are like a fortress in our

---

[116] Isaiah 26:3-4, NIV.
[117] Isaiah 26:3-4, RSV.
[118] Isaiah 26:3-4, The Living Bible.

lives. If we trust Him, we can know peace.

Many people feel worried and anxious because they are uncertain what the future holds. But we can place our complete trust in God because He is in control, and He knows the future. God understands the "big picture" that we cannot see. If we fully trust God and know that He will never leave us, then we have nothing to fear.

Another important lesson I have learned about peace is the importance of spiritual rest. Jesus understood this well and offered these words of encouragement to his followers:

> *"Come to me, all who labor and are heavy laden, and I will give you rest. Take my yoke upon you and learn from me; for I am gentle and lowly in heart, and you will find rest for your souls. For my yoke is easy, and my burden is light."*[119]

I believe that Jesus perceived the weight of the people's stress caused by oppressive religious legalism. The people were overwhelmed and exhausted trying to live up to the strict expectations the law imposed. Jesus' ministry and message were all about God's grace, not legal perfection, nor earning one's salvation. Jesus reassured the people that He could provide rest for their souls.

We are called to live in freedom. We can experience the peace that comes with being free from the crushing burden of trying to earn God's favor through good deeds. Spiritual rest brings peace, not guilt.

No one ever said that life was supposed to be easy. Becoming a believer in Christ does not exempt us from disappointments, tragedy, or heartache. However, we have hope, which enables us to endure the difficulties that come our way. God is alongside us to give us His strength, wisdom, and guidance. We do not have to worry or panic because we can trust that God will help us through whatever circumstances befall us. We may not survive our

---
[119] Matthew 11:28-30.

tragedies in the way we imagined, but God will never abandon us. He will be with us throughout the journey.

During my life, when I have been at my lowest, I felt as though the ground was ripped out from under me. Life simply seemed to fall apart. Despite my downcast state, I still recognized the precious gift of peace—like focusing on that one object in the room during labor. This divine gift from God kept me strong and calm amid crisis and tragedy. I relied on His strength and His wisdom to pull me through life's most devastating circumstances. It was easy to take peace for granted when everything was going well, but peace became a life raft for me when I persevered through the darkest of storms I had ever known.

The gospel writers share many stories about the miraculous healings Jesus performed. There is a common refrain at the end of many of these accounts. Following the miracle, Jesus often said, "Your faith has made you well. Go in peace." Did you catch those last three words? Go in peace. Why do you think Jesus chose to share these words with someone he had just healed? I believe there are several reasons.

First, for the one who is seriously ill, peace is elusive. Anyone who has ever suffered with a chronic illness or endured a disability since birth understands how easy it is to concentrate all one's attention on the infirmity. Dealing with constant pain requires every ounce of energy a person possesses. It demands an inordinate amount of time and attention to research doctors, schedule appointments, attend doctor visits, travel back and forth to the hospital, explore rehabilitation facilities, and navigate insurance coverage. It is exhausting.

The gospel of Luke was written by a physician who understood the anguish and despair of physical illness. He shared a heart-wrenching story about a woman who had suffered for twelve years with a blood hemorrhage. She visited many doctors; yet none of them could heal her. The gospel writer Mark also wrote of this story, adding that the woman spent all the money she had, and instead of getting better, she grew worse. Imagine how hopeless she must have felt. She had tried everything. Her resources were depleted. Despite fighting for twelve years, she remained just as sick as she was when her illness began.

When the woman heard that Jesus was coming to her town, she decided she simply had to see him. A crowd surrounded Him, but she believed if she could get close enough to touch him that she would be healed. As weak as she was, she crawled on her hands and knees beneath the crowd to make her way to Jesus. She could not get close enough to touch him directly, but she bravely reached out and brushed the hem of His garment. She was instantly healed. Jesus suddenly stopped because he recognized that power had flowed through Him. He asked, "Who touched me?" The woman stood before Jesus, trembled with fear, and told him the truth. He lovingly responded, "Daughter, your faith has made you well. Go in peace."[120]

I am certain that Jesus' blessing and gift of peace transformed her life as much as her physical healing. She was freed from the prison of a chronic illness to live with peace in her soul. As she went forward to spread the good news, I am sure she spoke passionately of Jesus, the man who brought restoration not only to her body but to her spirit as well.

Once we experience authentic spiritual peace, we never want to live without it again. The Apostle Paul knew the value of peace to sustain us through life's travails. While he was serving a two-year prison sentence in Rome, Paul wrote to the members of a church he founded in Philippi. Of all the churches he established, none was as near to Paul's heart as the Philippians. Love and gratitude are seen everywhere within the pages of this Christian love letter. Paul encouraged his friends to stay strong, exhorting them:

> *"Have no anxiety about anything, but in everything by prayer and supplication with thanksgiving, let your requests be made known to God. And the peace of God, which passes all understanding, will keep your hearts and your minds in Christ Jesus."*[121]

---

[120] Luke 8:43-48; Mark 5:25-34.
[121] Philippians 4:6-7.

Paul knew that God's remarkable peace was what helped keep his heart and mind fixed upon the Lord even while behind bars. Despite his many challenging circumstances, Paul was able to wholly devote himself to the Lord, to do His work with devout commitment and unflagging fervor.

The search for spiritual peace is a wise pursuit. The disciple Peter lived an exceptional life. For a man who began life as a simple, hard-working fisherman, he went on to become one of the most instrumental leaders in the history of Christianity. He became head of the early church, and he is looked upon with great respect as the first pope.

Between Peter and Paul, they literally carried the gospel to the ends of the known world. Paul was called to reach out to the Gentiles, who were mostly pagans. Peter's calling was to the Jews. His challenges were immense, trying to convince God's people that Jesus was indeed the Messiah, the one promised for centuries. Peter's passion was to preach the gospel of Christ. He wrote in his second epistle, "May grace and peace be multiplied to you in the knowledge of God and of Jesus our Lord."[122] Peter was convinced that the more believers understood about God, the more familiar they became with His promises. This sharpened their thinking as they were saturated by the words of Jesus. This mysteriously multiplied grace and peace in their lives.

Peter also knew that the value of peace is priceless. I am sure he never forgot the dark moments of his triple denial of Christ. He never forgot the relief and joy of Jesus' forgiveness and restoration. Peter spent the rest of his life carrying the gospel, exhorting others to do whatever it took to know God's peace. In his later years, Peter gave the following advice, "Seek peace and pursue it over a lifetime."[123] For this cause, Peter died a martyr's death.

Believers are imbued with many talents and gifts. There is something very special about the individuals the Bible calls "peacemakers." I believe these people

---

[122] II Peter 1:2.
[123] I Peter 3:11.

live unselfish lives, dedicated to leading people to personal peace. They derive great joy in bringing people together who have previously been torn apart, and they work tirelessly to resolve conflict within the church, government, and families. In the Sermon on the Mount, Jesus praised these precious saints, proclaiming, "Blessed are the peacemakers, for they shall be called sons of God."[124] Those who promote the peace of God and work to instill it in others reflect our Heavenly Father.

John's oldest brother Tony, my beloved brother-in-law, is an extraordinarily gifted peacemaker. As the oldest of six children, he probably had a lot of opportunities to hone this skill when helping to solve squabbles among his siblings. As a brilliant surgeon, Tony counseled individuals who were seeking peace regarding their physical health. He is a natural born leader, and he understands the value that peace can play in our lives. His advice and counsel were invaluable to us as we struggled to make countless decisions about John's health. He knew that in our hearts we longed to have peace about the direction and course that John's treatment was taking. Tony knew we would have to live with the decisions we made.

God used Tony to gently and lovingly share the idea with John and me that it was perhaps time to seek out the expertise of another hospital, states away from where we lived. It was hard news to deliver, but over time, Tony led us to make the decision to fight to the end to save John's life. He also backed his advice with his time. Tony went with us via air ambulance and helped pave the way for us at the new institution to wage the toughest battle we had ever known. When we lost John, I knew we had tried everything humanly possible and that I could live the rest of my life with no regrets. The price tag of peace is priceless. As he was being used by God, Tony gave us that gift.

I want to close this chapter with a beautiful benediction from the book of Hebrews which I believe succinctly summarizes the Bible's insights on peace:

---

[124] Matthew 5:9.

"Now may the God of Peace who brought again from the dead our Lord Jesus, the great shepherd of the sheep, by the blood of the eternal covenant, equip you with everything good, that you may do His will, working in you that which is pleasing in His sight, through Jesus Christ, to whom be glory forever and ever."[125]

We worship the God of Peace. It is a treasure to know in our minds and hearts that we are living out God's will and purpose for our life. He provides everything good we need. As we stand firmly in this knowledge, contentment and peace overflow.

What does God want you to know about Him? That His peace is priceless. Seek His peace at all costs. The gift of contentment is a treasure.

---

[125] "Hebrews 13:20-21."

Questions for Reflection

* Describe your thoughts regarding the role that personal peace plays in your life.

* Have you had previous challenges in searching for peace of mind and heart? How did it impact you?

* The author shared the Bible story about the woman who suffered with a blood hemorrhage for twelve years. Can you relate to her predicament? What did her action reveal about her beliefs?

* Read Philippians 4:6-7. How does it illuminate your understanding of this passage knowing that the Apostle Paul wrote these words while in prison?

CHAPTER SIXTEEN

"I Want the Best for You"

What is it about being human that makes us all want to be right? No one ever seems to enjoy being wrong, whether it is in a spirited discussion or a complicated situation. Now that I am older, I have realized that in many areas of life there is no right or wrong. Sometimes it boils down to a preference, an opinion, or a variety of options.

Years ago, I heard a song written by Susan Ashton that spoke to this topic, "Agree to Disagree." Sometimes when we reach an impasse with someone we love, we simply do what the song says—we agree to disagree. We choose not to see eye to eye, but we accept that we will be in discord on a particular issue.

It would be nice if all concerns in life could be resolved like this, but they cannot. Sometimes, when it comes to big decisions, the kind that may have a major or lasting impact, we need more than ideas or opinions. We need wisdom. This is where the life of a believer gets exciting—for we are in relationship with God who is all-wise and all-knowing.

For centuries, theologians have searched the Scriptures, seeking the keys to unlocking the mysteries of God's wisdom. I believe trying to provide a tidy explanation of God's wisdom is like trying to explain the mystery of the Virgin Birth or that of the Trinity. It just cannot be done, nor perhaps should it be done. God's wisdom is mysterious because it encompasses so many of His other attributes and characteristics. We may not comprehend His wisdom, but we can assert that His wisdom is intertwined with His goodness.

What is it about God's wisdom that makes it such a precious, valuable gift in our lives?

God Sees the Big Picture

Often when we are weighed down by a frustrating situation, we are overwhelmed because we only possess partial information. We perceive the presence of a greater, more complicated predicament, but our lack of knowledge blinds us. This is where God's vision is invaluable. As the Creator of the Universe, He sees what we cannot. God knows the past, present, and future. He sees the end from the beginning.

In the book of Genesis, we meet a complex man named Joseph. He was the eleventh of twelve sons of Israel's patriarch Jacob. His many brothers were envious because Joseph was favored by his father who lavished him with a visible sign of his favoritism—a resplendent coat of many colors. The brothers' anger grew hot and serious, leading them to devise a wicked scheme. They sold Joseph into slavery for twenty pieces of silver to some travelers who took him to Egypt. They return home with his beautiful coat and tell their heartbroken father that Joseph had been killed by wild animals.

While in Egypt, Joseph has many frightening, harrowing experiences. Despite his fear and anger, he trusts that God continues to care for him. Joseph hopes and prays for God to rescue him from peril. Many years pass and Joseph eventually obtains a high position in the kingdom of the Pharaoh of Egypt. His keen administrative skills prompt him to acquire grain supplies that enable

Egypt to withstand a great famine. His brothers travel from Canaan to Egypt to obtain much-needed food for their survival during the famine. When they meet with him, they do not recognize Joseph. When he reveals to his brothers who he really is, they fall before him begging for forgiveness. He responds, "You intended to harm me, but God intended it for good, to accomplish what is now being done, the saving of many lives."[126] God saw the big picture when Joseph could not. He knew what was best for Joseph who helped save the nation of Egypt and his own family. God can use evil for good.

God Understands Short-term vs. Long-term

Delayed gratification is an important lesson that we all learn at some point in our lives. But even after we learn this strategy, it remains difficult to enact. It is just plain tough to choose between something that is good right now versus something that may be better later.

When we had infants, John and I were bound and determined to get them on a schedule to preserve our sanity. We knew the only way that would work for us was to let our babies cry in order to learn they could wait for their next feeding. At first, this was excruciating. We both wanted to leap out of bed, lift the baby out of the crib, and relieve him of his misery. After a couple of days, though, the baby started crying less and less. He learned he would have to wait to satisfy his hunger. Eventually, the baby began to soothe himself back to sleep. Voila! Baby on schedule. Happy parents! Delayed gratification can produce amazing rewards.

God knows that when we cry out to him for sudden relief—Lord, I want you to take this from me this very moment—that we are only thinking of our short-term need. He sees the potential of our long-term situation when we simply cannot.

---

[126] Genesis 50:20, NRV.

God Knows Us Better Than We Know Ourselves

Sometimes we think we can predict how we will react in a certain situation, but when the scenario occurs, we surprise ourselves with how we really respond. I have learned that God knows me better than I know myself. Because He made me, He knows my most intricate intellectual and emotional wirings, my psychological subtleties. He knows what I am capable of and what could become a breaking point for me.

I was involved in two serious romantic relationships before meeting John. But once we fell in love, I knew he was the only one for me. Since the moment we were married, I had a hidden fear of one day losing him. My love for him was so fierce and deep that I knew in my heart I simply could not withstand life without him by my side. I naively guessed it was an issue that was likely sixty or seventy years in our future; yet it still secretly plagued me. I used to pray that I would die before John because I knew he could handle losing a spouse more readily than I could. He was so strong. I assumed I would just crumble and be completely broken.

But God knows me better than I know myself. He knew my future pain would be the greatest struggle of my life, but He knew He would bring healing to me over time. God knew all along that he would lead me to a place where grief could eventually reside in my heart, and He knew he would ultimately bring me to a place of peace.

I lost John when he was fifty-nine years old. We had dreamed of retirement together. We used to talk about the many places where we longed to travel when we had the time and freedom to explore. That was not to be. John worked diligently for his entire career but did not get to know the joy of retirement after all his labors. That broke my heart. When I turned sixty, it was hard for me to realize I had surpassed an age that John would never know.

Yet, God is faithful. He knows me better than I know myself. He knew I would grow in ways I never imagined, despite realizing my greatest fear. I never guessed I could learn to live with my loss of John, despite the immense hole left in my life. I never envisioned how God would sustain me and give me the courage and strength to love and support my three children through the loss of their father.

Immediately following the loss of John, his youngest brother Bill, my beloved brother-in-law, came to my rescue. Being married to a CPA all those years meant that I depended solely on John for all financial and technical aspects of our life. I had no idea when he paid our bills, how he negotiated the refinancing of our home, nor how he impeccably prepared and filed our taxes on time each year. I was spoiled rotten and incredibly naïve. John used to tease and say, "Kim thinks credit cards are like Monopoly money," if that gives you any indication of my knowledge of finances.

Bill was sent straight from God to help me in this area of great weakness. He has always been there for me and the kids. I believe he made a promise to his big brother to help look after us, and his devotion and faithfulness are unwavering. I would feel lost without his love, support, and tangible help. About two years after our loss, I retired from my career as a marketing director for a law firm. I was in a funk—I felt like I was drifting aimlessly, being blown by the wind. I thought I would feel this way for the rest of my life. Bill sensed my restlessness. He stopped me in my tracks one day when he said, "Kim, God is not finished with you yet. He still has a plan for your life. Maybe you will even get back to writing your book."

Despite all I had endured, Bill was right—God still had a plan for my life. Even though my life did not turn out the way I hoped or planned, God never gives up on us. I can depend upon His love for me and His wisdom to know me better than I know myself.

God Always Wants What Is Best

In His imminent wisdom and goodness, God knows there are many avenues available to solve our problems, heal our wounds, improve our attitudes, and bring harmony to our relationships. But He doesn't always want what is simply good for us—He wants what is best for us. God sometimes protects us from accepting what is good because He knows if we are willing to wait upon His perfect timing, we will be open to receive what is even better.

God's wisdom is mysterious and complex, but we know His wisdom is part of who He is. To know God intimately is to accept that He is all-wise. Step by step, as we mature in our faith, we begin to trust and lean upon His wisdom to guide us. "To God belong wisdom and power; counsel and understanding are His."[127] God's wisdom encompasses more than His knowledge; it also includes the skillfulness and infinite power to formulate and implement plans in the most effective manner. He prepares the best solutions and brings them to fruition by the most perfect means.

Do we sometimes doubt God's wisdom? If so, we need to admit that what we really doubt is God's capability to know everything and His power to do anything. We fret that His knowledge and understanding are not good enough for us. We would do well in these moments to remember, "It is He who made the earth by His power, who established the world by His wisdom, and by His understanding stretched out the heavens."[128] In God's wisdom He created a world by a spoken word, became flesh through earthly birth by a virgin, and allowed the precious blood of Jesus to serve in the place of our own to redeem us. If we ask God to teach us to trust in His wisdom, He will show us countless examples of how His wisdom has guided His actions since the beginning of time.

"O the depth of the riches and wisdom and knowledge of God! How unsearchable are His judgments and how inscrutable His ways!"[129]

---

[127] Job 12:13.
[128] Jeremiah 10:12.
[129] Romans 11:33.

Many American presidents have written in their memoirs how much they learned to depend upon God's wisdom while in office. I cannot imagine the stress that accompanies this position, but I can only believe it would be foolish to lead the nation without trusting in God's wisdom. While in office, President George W. Bush shared in a speech, "We can trust in that greater power who guides the unfolding of the years. And, in all that is to come, we can know that His purposes are just and true."[130] Similarly, President Barack Obama remarked in a speech:

> *In the wake of failures and disappointments I have questioned what God had in store for me and been reminded that God's plans for us may not always match our own short-sighted desires. And let me tell you, these past two years, they have deepened my faith. The presidency has a funny way of making a person feel the need to pray. Abe Lincoln said, as many of you know, "I have been driven to my knees many times by the overwhelming conviction that I had no place else to go."*[131]

We may never become a world leader, but we are foolish if we pass up the opportunity to go to the best place we can for wisdom—straight to God. "Make your ears attentive to wisdom and incline your heart to understanding."[132] We need to approach God with the eyes to see and the ears to hear the wisdom and direction He has for us.

Have you ever encountered the wise counsel of a fellow believer? This is one way God frequently endows our lives with wisdom. I cannot count the times

---

[130] President George W. Bush, "Third Presidential State of the Union Address," transcript of speech delivered at The House of Representatives Chamber of the United States Capitol, January 20, 2004.

[131] President Barack Obama, "Remarks by the President at the National Prayer Breakfast," transcript of speech delivered at the Washington Hilton, Washington DC, February 3, 2011.

[132] Proverbs 2:6.

that a young child, a good friend, or a seasoned elder has spoken God's truth to me.

Our three children, John Jr., Mark and Laura, are now young adults, each with their own personalities and admirable journeys of faith. They each have a unique relationship with the Lord. I have learned many wise ideas and sound theological concepts from them. When they were young, they looked at many things and asked, "Why?" Now, as adults, they look at many things and ask, "Why not?" Their candor and unpretentious attitudes refresh me and enlighten me with God's wisdom.

"If any of you lacks wisdom, he should ask God, who gives generously to all without finding fault and it will be given to him."[133] When I ask God for wisdom, which I frequently do, I always hear the same response. His sweet voice whispers deep within my spirit, Study my Word. Study my Word. What wisdom I have gained, and had the privilege to share with others, has come from the truth gleaned by delving into the Scriptures. His truth is there for a purpose: to be grasped, acknowledged, and applied to our everyday encounters.

"The wisdom from above is first pure, then peaceable, gentle, open to reason, full of mercy and good fruits, without uncertainty or insincerity."[134] I use this as a litmus test when I receive advice from other people or when I believe I have heard God's voice. If the ideas do not align completely with this description of wisdom, then I discount it. This is how I can know if the information is truly from God.

At the end of the thirteenth chapter of the book of I Corinthians, the Apostle Paul's well-known treatise on love, he tucks in a metaphor I can relate to, "For now we see in a mirror dimly, but then face to face. Now I know in part; then I shall understand fully, even as I have been fully understood."[135]

---

[133] James 1:5.
[134] James 3:17.
[135] I Corinthians 13:12.

The mysteries of God's wisdom may seem like a dim reflection until I am one day with God in Heaven. By His grace, I have learned that His wisdom, knowledge and strength will continue to sustain me.

What does God want you to know about Him? That He wants the best for you. Trust His wisdom. Be confident of His vision. Depend upon His strength. There is no better way to live.

Questions for Reflection

* What is it about God's wisdom that makes it such a precious, valuable gift in our lives?

* How does it change your relationship with God to know that He sees the big picture in your life?

* The author asserts that God understands short-term vs. long-term situations in our lives. How can this be a benefit to us?

* What ways can you trust God's wisdom and be confident of His vision for your life?

Afterword

This book began as a nugget of an idea for a Bible Study I conceived in 2012. A year later, I created a ten-week study class for a group of adults at my beloved church, Hyde Park Presbyterian, in Tampa, Florida. I am grateful to this collection of curious, intelligent Christian friends whose hearts are pure in their quest for knowledge and truth. They taught me more than I could ever imagine teaching them through their insights and heartfelt questions that prompted us to explore the depths of God and His wonders together.

A special thanks goes to Kelly Beiro, one of the friends in the original Bible study, the first person to ever say to me, "I think you should write a book about these concepts." To my friends Jett and Steven Tanner, also in the original study, much thanks for their never-ending cups of coffee and encouragement before each Sunday morning class.

Despite working long hours in my full-time marketing career, and caring for my aging mother afflicted with Alzheimer's, I wrote as often as I could until January 2016 when John received his diagnosis. For nearly two years we battled his illness until he died in 2017. I struggled with our loss, and it wasn't until 2020 when I felt strong enough emotionally to revisit this writing project. It was with some trepidation I wondered if these foundational principles I believed about God and His nature would stand the test of time. Would these ideas still ring true despite all I had experienced? Did these aspects of God continue to hold up as reliable in my life and in my walk of faith?

It is now 2022, ten years after God first planted the seeds of these concepts in my heart and mind. Over the past decade, my life has changed dramatically, and I have known profound loss. I not only lost John, but I also lost my mother, my brother-in-law Steve, my brother Rick, and my mother-in-law Monk as well.

I have learned the harsh reality that life is hard. But, upon returning to these original seeds of truth, my heart rejoiced to discover that each one held up as valid and strong. In fact, as I confronted and reexamined each dimension of God's personality, my faith increased and my commitment to His truth became more fervent.

I owe a debt of immense gratitude to the many family members and friends who have encouraged me throughout the process of writing this book. Their loving support has helped me cross the finish line.

Much thanks to Trudy Hale, and her beautiful writer's retreat, The Porches, in Norwood, Virginia, where I had the privilege to stow away and write my heart out over three separate visits over the course of eight years. Heartfelt thanks to Mark and Anne Kaiser, part of my "chosen family," for the gracious time spent at their lovely farm in Liberty, South Carolina where I enjoyed a full month of writing during a beautiful autumn season. A special thanks to Sandra Santos for watching over my home in Tampa while I was away on writing treks, never once letting any of my plants die.

I am grateful to David Ferris for his expert editing, keen discernment and warm sense of humor. I can't wait to work with him again.

Praise God from whom all blessings flow.

—Kim Harvey Brannan
   March 2022